The *Apocalypse* in *African-American* Fiction

THE APOCALYPSE

IN AFRICAN-AMERICAN FICTION

Maxine Lavon Montgomery

University Press of Florida

Gainesville Tallahassee Tampa Boca Raton
Pensacola Orlando Miami Jacksonville

01   00   99   98   97   96   6   5   4   3   2   1

Library of Congress Cataloging-in-Publication Data

Montgomery, Maxine Lavon, 1959-
The Apocalypse in African-American fiction/
Maxine Lavon Montgomery
p. cm.
Includes bibliographical references and index.
ISBN 0-8130-1389-5 (alk. paper)
1. American fiction—Afro-American authors—
History and criticism. 2. Apocalyptic literature—
History and criticism. 3. Christianity and
literature—United States. 4. Fiction—Religious
aspects—Christianity. 5. End of the world in
literature. 6. Afro-Americans in literature. I. Title.
PS374.A65M66   1966
813.009'38—dc 20   95-36850

The University Press of Florida is the scholarly
publishing agency for the State University System
of Florida, comprised of Florida A & M University,
Florida Atlantic University, Florida International
University, Florida State University, University of
Central Florida, University of Florida, University of
North Florida, University of South Florida, and
University of West Florida.

University Press of Florida
15 Northwest 15th Street
Gainesville, FL 32611

CONTENTS

PREFACE

I became aware of the use of apocalypse among African-American novelists while enrolled in a graduate course on postmodern black fiction at the University of Illinois-Champaign. Not only did I notice that the authors whose works we read frequently turned to biblical apocalyptics in giving form and essence to their works, it became clear to me that they did so with a rhetorical emphasis that differed from that of their American counterparts.

This book reflects what has become an ongoing interest on my part in the close relationship between biblical texts and African-American fictional discourse. Apocalypse, an idiom that is central to the black literary tradition, seemed the best starting point for scholarly inquiry into the ways in which the Bible has influenced black writing. It is my hope that this book will help to lay the critical groundwork for further study of the connections between Scriptural texts and African-American literature.

My primary purpose in writing is to reveal the uniqueness of the image of apocalypse in African-American fiction. Because African Americans have been excluded from full participation in America's social, political, and economic mainstream, they have been forced to develop a theological perspective at odds with that of White America. From the point of view of the dispossessed masses, the end of the world suggests a welcomed end to all forms of oppression and the beginning of a new era of equality—in this life more so than in the next one.

In undertaking this enterprise, I wish to acknowledge the assistance of those who helped to make this book a reality: Chester J. Fontenot II and Emily Watts, for offering criticisms throughout; the Florida Endowment Fund for Higher Education, for awarding me a McKnight Junior Faculty Fellowship while I wrote and conducted research; Fred Standley, Joseph McElrath, Hunt Hawkins, and Anne Rowe, for reading portions of the book-in-progress; and, the late Richard Kenneth Barksdale, my mentor and dissertation director, whose fatherly wisdom, guidance, and encouragement inspired me to persevere.

Finally, since portions of this book have appeared elsewhere as articles, I wish to thank the editors of *College Language Association Journal* and *Black American Literature Forum* for permission to reprint. Chapter 2, "Richard Wright, *Native Son*," appeared in *College Language Association Journal* 34, no. 4 (June 1991): 453–66; chapter 6, "Toni Morrison, *Sula*," appeared in *African-American Review/Black American Literature Forum* 23, no. 1 (Spring 1989): 127–37; and chapter 7, "Gloria Naylor, *The Women of Brewster Place*," appeared in *College Language Association Journal* 36, no. 1 (September 1992): 1–11.

The *Apocalypse* in *African-American* Fiction

Write the things which thou hast seen, and the things which are, and the things which shall be hereafter: The mystery of the seven stars which thou sawest in my right hand, and the seven golden candlesticks. The seven stars are the angels of the seven churches; and the seven candlesticks which thou sawest are the seven churches.

Revelation 1:19–20

Oh-o-oh, sinner,
Where will you stand,
In that great day when God's a-going to rain down fire?
Oh, you gambling man—where will you stand?
You whore-mongering man—where will you stand?
Liars and backsliders—where will you stand,
In that great day when God's a-going to rain down fire?

James Weldon Johnson, "The Judgment Day"

The unknown folk bards and the conscious, creative artists of black American culture, on the other hand, have turned to a discussion of the last acts and objects in a different mood, for blacks have long believed that their dignity, status, and freedom as a people are dependent upon the descent of an apocalypse on a corrupt and oppressive white world, and a number of works in the black American literary tradition give forceful expression to this belief.

Houston Baker, *Long Black Song*

INTRODUCTION

When President George Bush addressed the nation in the aftermath of the 1991 Gulf War, his phrase "the new world order" referred to the system of government to emerge after the crisis. The new world order Mr. Bush envisioned was a multinational one to be built upon militaristic aggression, political strength, and world domination cloaked in the guise of democracy. These catchwords validated the notion of manifest destiny present in the national psyche. But when African-American leaders spoke of the crisis, their rhetorical emphasis stressed America's hypocrisy in intervening in a foreign country's dilemma while neglecting the more pressing social, economic, and political problems confronting black citizens at home.

A result of these two divergent political agendas—one predominantly white, the other primarily black—is the identification of conflicting notions of what constitutes an apocalyptic vision. This book's primary purpose is to substantiate the assertion that not only is there an apocalypticism in the African-American tradition, but also to show how African-American novelists have used the image of the end of the world, creating a variant that is distinct to black fictional discourse. In that literary tradition apocalypse is a mode of expression revealing a concern with the end of an oppressive sociopolitical system and the establishment of a new world order where racial justice prevails. In apocalypse, then, there is evidence of the crisis-ridden African-American experience: the movement from country to city, the change from a rural or agrarian to an urban or industrialized environment, and once history disappointed the hope for progress, the search for a tenable response to continued racist oppression.

Much of what constitutes an apocalypse in the African-American tradition remains encoded in a rich oral tradition. This is the major premise underlying Houston Baker's seminal essay, "Freedom and Apocalypse: A Thematic Approach to Black Expression," which offers a basis for theorizing about the use of the idiom (*Long Black Song* 42–57). That language occupies a key place in the history of black writing should come as no surprise, however, for the slave narratives contain numerous examples of the attempt on the part of slaves to master language in both its oral and written forms. One is reminded of Frederick Douglass's having tricked unsuspecting whites into teaching him to read and write. What Douglass and other slaves realized was that their individual and collective destinies, as slaves and freedmen, were relevant to the manipulation of language. In his assessment of the concerns that distinguish the canon, Bernard Bell mentions the apocalypse in conjunction with the black vernacular tradition:

> the tradition of the Afro-American novel is dominated by the struggle for freedom from all forms of oppression and by the personal odyssey to realize the full potential of one's complex bicultural identity as an Afro-American. This archetypal journey—deriving its sociocultural consciousness from the group experience of black Americans and its mythopoeic force from the interplay of Eurocentric and Afrocentric mythological systems—begins in physical or psychological bondage and ends in some ambiguous form of deliverance or vision of a new world of mutual respect and justice for peoples of color. In short, if there is an Afro-American canonical story, it is the quest, frequently with apocalyptic undertones, for freedom, literacy, and wholeness—personal and communal—grounded in social reality and ritualized in symbolic acts of Afro-American speech, music, and religion. (341–42)

What Bell's comments imply, and what this study argues more explicitly, is that African-American novelists are not imitators of an apocalyptic tradition spawned by whites; rather, they are creators of an apocalyptic story that is their own.[1] An investigation of the apocalypse in black fictional discourse must therefore begin with a consideration of the forms of cultural expression indigenous to African Americans, not with a focus on that of whites; it must begin within the tradition, not outside of it.

Writing an apocalyptic novel is a socially symbolic act with a meaning often hidden from the eyes of those outside the culture, because the novelist uses language in an effort to inscribe a future that challenges the beliefs present in the American mythos. In the African-American tradition, language is not neutral but is dictated by sociocultural precedents. Susan Willis points out that when the black writer takes the materials of folk culture and subjects them to fiction, a system of meaning and telling that originates in the dominant culture, she is engaged in "an enterprise fraught with contradiction" (69–70). Those contradictions manifest themselves in the tension between the dictates of formal, written English, the system from which the American apocalypse derives, and the oral, unwritten language of the black masses. Ralph Ellison's discussion of his use of folklore suggests the importance of folk material to black fictional discourse:

> For us the question should be, What are the specific forms of that humanity, and what in our background is worth preserving or abandoning. The clue to this can be found in folklore, which offers the first drawings of any group's character. It preserves mainly those situations which have repeated themselves again and again in the history of any given group. It describes those rites, manners, customs, and so forth, which insure the good life, or destroy it; and it describes those boundaries of feeling, thought and action which that particular group has found to be the limitation of the human condition. It projects this wisdom in symbols which express the group's will to survive; it embodies those values by which the group lives and dies. These drawings may be crude but they are nonetheless profound in that they represent the group's attempt to humanize the world. It's no accident that great literature, the products of individual artists, is erected on this humble base. (*Shadow and Act* 170–71)

And in "Blueprint For Negro Literature," Richard Wright offers a formula for black literature that points to folk material as a valuable source in reshaping reality along new lines:

> Negro folklore contains, in a measure that puts to shame more deliberate forms of expression, the collective sense of the Negroes' life in America. Let those who shy at the nationalist implications of Negro life look at this body of folklore, living and powerful, which rose out of a unified sense of a common life and a common fate. Here are those vital beginnings of that recognition of value in life as it is lived that marks the emergence of a new culture in the shell of the old. And at the moment that starts, at the moment a people begin to realize a meaning in their suffering, the civilization which engenders that suffering is doomed. Negro folklore remains the Negro writer's most powerful weapon, a weapon which he must sharpen for the hard battles

looming ahead, battles which will test a people's faith in themselves. (*Amistad 2:Writings on Black History Culture* 8)

At the turn of the century W. E. B. Du Bois articulated the essence of the psychological dilemma of African Americans when he made mention of the sense of "two-ness" blacks experience in a racially divided country (45). America is comprised of two societies, not one, and a central struggle in which African Americans find themselves is one for wholeness, selfhood, and identity. For Abdul R. JanMohamed, the Manichaean sociopolitical relation between the colonizer and the colonized illustrates the reality impinging upon the novel and gives a clue to understanding the novelists' political concerns. "The black writer finds that colonialist praxis and literature promote a negative, derogatory image of Africa and its inhabitants," he suggests, "and thus he is motivated to attempt a correction of that image through a symbolic, literary recreation of an alternate, more just picture of indigenous cultures" (8).

Because the fictional world of the novel is multidimensional and mirrors the one blacks confront in society, Henry Louis Gates's suggestion that black texts are double-voiced, with not only white and black novels as literary antecedents but modes of figuration from the black vernacular tradition, seems justified. Thus, there is a peculiar dualism at work in the black literary apocalypse. On one level, there is a voice that affirms the popular nineteenth-century ideal of America as the new world Garden of Eden, a belief in Adamic innocence, and manifest destiny. At the same time, however, there is also a dissenting voice, a timeless, enduring, testifying voice that speaks of achieving in spite of America's failed promises.[2] It is the presence of this dualistic voice and its inherent irony that distinguishes the black literary apocalypse. In order to understand the nature of this voice it is necessary to consider the religious discourse emanating from the church. Whatever is black about black literature is to be found not just in the vernacular tradition, as Gates astutely observes, but in the aspect of that tradition relevant to the existence of a unique theological perspective.

The image of the end of the world is present in the novels of authors whose orientation is not specifically Christian, as in the case of the atheistic Richard Wright. It also appears in a novel by James Baldwin who, in spite of being raised within the church, is openly critical of that institution. In an apocalyptic novel the author responds to the crisis of the times, whether it is world war or sociopolitical injustice. But he [re]writes the apocalypse from the self-conscious position of one who is outside of the bedlam, much like Ralph Ellison's invisible narrator safe in an underground retreat during the Harlem race riot. By allowing his narrator to offer a verbal account of the chaos, Ellison makes an important although unacknowledged contribution to an understanding of the literary apocalypse.

One of the greatest difficulties involved in this study stems from the ambiguities surrounding the term *apocalypse* and its long and sometimes confusing history in ancient and modern eras. *Apocalypse* comes from the Greek word *apokalupsis*, which means a disclosure of something previously hidden or unknown. Like the Latin term *revelatio* from which Revelation, the chief apocalyptic text of the New Testament canon, acquires its name, it involves an unveiling of truth. The term is to be distinguished from eschatology, the branch of Christian theology dealing with the last things—heaven, hell, death, and judgment. It was in Judaism during the reign of Antiochus Epiphanes (175–163 B.C.) that a literary genre of the apocalyptic emerged.[3] The writing of the literature was restricted to the circle of the wise—the learned, those who claimed to have a special revelation from God. In its early manifestations the literature was strictly prophetic, involving encouragement for the Jews during successive phases of their history. Not surprisingly, such writing enjoyed a wide popular appeal to the Jewish nation. During the time that the literature flourished, the Jews were experiencing persecution from corrupt political rulers whose laws were at variance with orthodox religious belief. Although fear and despair were at their height, apocalypse served as a source of encouragement for these oppressed people of God. They could endure suffering because they knew an end was close at hand.

What is particularly relevant to this study is the close relationship between the production of apocalypse and the sociopolitical condition of the oppressed Jews. Jewish apocalyptists believed that there was a moral factor involved in the world and that those who violated God's authority would be deposed. D. S. Russell comments on the milieu that gave rise to apocalyptics: "It was an era of severe testing—of persecution, suffering and death—when the hearts of the faithful longed passionately for the breaking in of God upon human affairs and the destruction of the wicked. These books reflect in a poignant and dramatic way the response of a deeply religious people to the terrible pressures and persecutions of their time" (5). Jewish sages thus wrote with a certain fervor born from their sense of destiny as God's chosen people in hopes of restoring the feeling of nationhood that then current political systems were bent on destroying.

Jewish apocalyptists felt that the king or the state was the arch enemy of orthodox faith and was to be opposed. It was during the early phases of Judaism that Antiochus IV adopted the title "God Manifest" and coerced his subjects into worshiping him. Russell asserts that it was probably one of the Party of Hasidim who wrote Daniel, the first Jewish apocalyptic text in the Old Testament canon. The book, which is addressed to the Jews in Babylonian captivity, exhorted them to hold on to their faith in light of the coming of the Messiah. In the end, corrupt rulers would be judged and the faithful among God's people rewarded.

R. H. Charles suggests that it was on the apocalyptic side of Judaism that Christianity evolved (23). The long delay in the Parousia coupled with the increasing deterioration of moral values resulted in a literature that ceased to be exclusively prophetic and became concerned instead with impending doom and destruction—the cataclysmic end of the world. Hence, from apocalyptic eschatology the modern usage of the term derived. Not only is there evidence of a concern with the end of the world in Old Testament scriptures—Ezekiel, Daniel, Joel, and Zechariah—but also in the earliest Christian writings in the Gospels.

Revelation, the last book in the New Testament canon, is a cryptic book of image-symbols, mysterious voices and visions, and Old Testament allusions. The ostensible author of the text is the Apostle John, exiled on the Isle of Patmos, who records the message of God addressed to seven churches in Roman Asia. Here, all the principal ingredients constituting apocalypse are present: series of sevens; the tribulation saints; the rise and reign of the Beast and false prophet; the appearance of the Lamb; the Battle of Armageddon and the millennium that follows; and the final judgment and the coming of the holy city, the New Jerusalem. During his panoramic vision the author John is translated through time and space from earth to heaven, but the revelation he receives is strictly historical. He is commanded to write "the things which thou hast seen," "the things which are" and "the things which shall be hereafter" (Revelation 1:19).

What he foresees are the events leading to the Second Coming of Christ and the end of the age. Relevant to such a vision is that in the Gospels Jesus discourages hope for a quick deliverance and directs attention to the signs preceding His return—wars, international unrest, famines, pestilences, persecutions, and false Christs: "For many shall come in my name, saying, I am Christ; and shall deceive many. And ye shall hear of wars and rumors of wars; see that ye be not troubled; for all these things must come to pass, but the end is not yet. For nation shall rise against nation, and kingdom against kingdom; and there shall be famines, and pestilences, and earth-quakes, in divers places. All these are the beginning of sorrows" (Matthew 24:7). Thus, Revelation offers a sense of resolution to history's unfolding drama, even as it points to a transcendent future beyond the chaos and turmoil of this present world system. It concludes with a glowing, final portrait of renewal and restoration: a new heaven and earth and the marriage between the Lamb and the church.

A possible reason for the fascination by the literary imagination with the apocalypse is that the event satisfies the need for order during chaotic times. This assertion is the basis for Frank Kermode's theorizing about fictional endings in relation to apocalypse itself. While the end has lost its imminence, he writes, it is nonetheless immanent (25). For the writer who stands in the middle of time desiring to make sense out of life, apocalypse offers a necessary concord between beginning, middle, and end. At the same time, however, the writer fears fictional endings because they suggest his own mortality. The writer thus fictionalizes the end while resisting its strict finality.

Northrup Frye considers the Bible as a dialectical progression—a revelation with seven main phases which culminate in apocalypse. More than any other scholar, it is Frye whose insights have contributed most to the understanding of the influence of the Bible on Western art and literature. He sees Revelation as a progression of antitypes, a mosaic of allusions to Old Testament Scripture, and divides apocalypse into two phases: the panoramic apocalypse, in which the tensions present in a fallen world remain, and a second, participating apocalypse, in which there is resolution and closure. "In this second life the creator-creature, divine-human antithetical tension has ceased to exist, and the sense of the transcendent person and the split of subject and object no longer limit our vision" (*The Great Code* 139–46).

Apocalypse in the African-American tradition evolved because of the contradictions between America's democratic ideals and the daily realities confronting the majority of African Americans. It reflects a people's response to the paradoxes of their times. From slavery and its aftermath there emerged a large body of folk material revealing an imaginative concern with Judeo-Christian eschatology among rural blacks, even as they attempted to adjust to life in the New World. Whether as the etiological animal tale involving a trickster figure whose acts of treachery result in a temporary overthrow of the white power structure, or as spirituals such as "Go Down Moses," which appears at the beginning of the following chapter, or as the folk preacher's creative rendering of the Last Judgment, the contributions of the folk artists of the past to African-American cultural expression indicate much more than just a superficial interest in what the Bible posits as the end of the world. In the early African-American imagination the event signals both the destruction of the oppressive systems of white society, including the one from which formal, written English originates, and a return to a prelapsarian existence in which oral, not written, discourse functions as the predominant mode of expression. If the thesis which E. Franklin Frazier expounds is valid, there is no such thing as an indigenous black form of expression, since the African accommodation to life in America tended to inhibit the transfer of traditional culture and beliefs. In *The Negro Church in America*, Frazier asserts that the manner in which Africans were captured, enslaved, and introduced into the plantation regime necessitated their abandonment of their own language and the adoption of that of whites (3).

Frazier's thesis is in sharp contrast with that of John Blassingame, Melville J. Herskovitz, Lawrence Levine, and Albert Raboteau, all of whom agree that vestiges of traditional African culture not only survived the grueling ordeal of the middle passage but are present in modified form in African-American culture and society.[4] Nevertheless, Frazier seems accurate in his observation that the black church offered a new basis for social cohesion in the antebellum South, and that is certainly a most valuable contribution to the understanding of black religious life in America. It was the church, an institution that originated and continues to exist outside of white society, that helped to foster the development of that language system resulting in apocalypse. Through a focus on the rich oral tradition emanating from this institution the subtleties of language use among the folk is apparent.

The slave masters used the Bible as part of the slavemaking process. Portions of Scripture pertaining to the Curse of Ham, the Pauline injunction regarding the duties of slaves to their masters, and the promise of an otherworldly heaven became texts that were to keep slaves in their places. Some slaves did embrace the version of Christianity designed to divert their attention away from achieving freedom in this life in exchange for a reward in an otherworldly heaven, but the prevalence of slave revolts and other more subtle forms of resistance on the plantation proves that there was a more radical interpretation of the Bible. Indeed, if there is a passage of Scripture that indicates the nature of society for African Americans, it is not one that stresses the comforts of life in Eden; it is one that speaks of alienation similar to that of Old Testament Jews in Babylonian exile: "How shall we sing the Lord's song in a strange Land?" (Psalms 137:4).

The slaves' ability to perceive the difference between true Christianity and the distorted version of it the slave masters presented allowed them to infuse biblical texts with new meaning. They therefore reinterpreted the Bible in terms relevant to their own reality. Raboteau delves deeply into slave life in an exploration of the role the Scriptures played in fueling the black hope for liberation: "The story of Israel's exodus from Egypt helped make it possible for the slaves to project a future radically different from their present. From other parts of the Bible, especially the prophetic and apocalyptic books, the slaves drew descriptions which gave form, and thus, assurance to their anticipation of deliverance" (312). Christianity was double-edged in the slaves' lives. On the one hand, whites used it as part of a system designed to render blacks docile, obedient, and complacent; on the other, blacks wielded it creatively in the ongoing struggle for nationhood.

The African-American search for liberation thus exists outside of the social mainstream. An example of this is present in the spirituals. Although Frazier contends that they are otherworldly in nature, Frederick Douglass speaks of them as complex cultural codes with a meaning accessible only to oppressed slaves. Douglass credits the music with inspiring his desire for freedom—in this life, not in the next (13–15). Something of this same perspective on the spirituals figures into W. E. B. Du Bois's perceptive discussion of them as sorrow songs chronicling the peculiarities of black life in white America (264–76). Du Bois's argument that folk artists have made an invaluable contribution to American society and culture is based on the continuities between traditional African culture and that of African Americans. He mentions the characteristic change biblical texts undergo once they enter the mouth of the unlettered slave. Du Bois concludes that blacks did not mimic American forms of music but created an original music expressive of the timelessness of their experience.

It is James Weldon Johnson whose discussion of the spirituals offers a most persuasive argument on behalf of the existence of a distinctly black language usage (11–50). Johnson focuses his discussion on the aesthetics of the spirituals—their form, style, and poetry. He traces the familiar call-and-response pattern present in the music to the African chant, which also makes use of this form. While Johnson concedes that the process of Americanization was likely to have resulted in the loss of a traditional African language, he also makes mention of the dialect slaves employed in communicating with each other and the slave master. The slaves' composition of the spirituals involved a fusion of a simplified English eliminating secondary moods and tenses with King James English and the phraseology of Old Testament prophets. Even though the unknown bards of the past drew upon biblical texts in the composition of the spirituals, then, they interjected into those texts distinct emotions and experiences. As a result, familiar biblical stories become more vivid and immediate. "Slaves simply refused to be uncritical recipients of a religion defined and controlled by white intermediaries and interpreters," Lawrence Levine notes in *Black Culture and Black Consciousness*. "No matter how respectfully and attentively they might listen to the white preachers, no matter how well they might sing the traditional hymns, it was their own preachers and their own songs that stirred them the most" (44).

More than any other aspect of the spirituals, it is the slaves' conception of heaven that speaks of this original reinterpretation of biblical texts. The slaves' mythological perspective was one that stressed beginnings in Africa, not America, and *heaven* ultimately signaled the symbolic recovery of a mythic past characterized by cultural, social, political, and economic freedom. Among oppressed slaves, heaven could refer to parts of the urban North, Canada, or even Africa, just as it could point to an otherworldly existence.[5] There was no dichotomy between the secular and spiritual, and time was not strictly linear but recursive, as is the case in some traditional African societies where death is not final; it is merely one stage in a rite of passage leading to a reunion with one's ancestors. John Mbiti's pioneering studies of traditional African religion emphasize the circular world view that distinguishes the African cosmology. He focuses on the language and mythology of the Akamba and notes that among them the future in the linear sense is nonexistent. Their many myths are primarily concerned with the past and their language excludes verb tenses expressive of future events (*New Testament Eschatology in an African Background* 24–27). According to Mbiti, in traditional African religion "There is no messianic hope or apocalyptic vision with God stepping in at some future moment to bring about a radical reversal of man's normal life. God is not pictured in an ethical-spiritual relationship with man. Man's acts of worship and turning to God are pragmatic and utilitarian rather than spiritual or mystical" (*African Religions and Philosophy* 6). Mircea Eliade's study of eschatology is dependent on his familiar thesis concerning the circularity of time in non-Western culture and society. Among those outside the West, Eliade argues, the end of the world has occurred in the past and will be repeated to a greater or lesser degree in the future (54).

In the African-American tradition, the Bible is a text that assumes meaning derived from a black theological perspective. Because of the blurred distinction between the secular and spiritual, between the past, present, and future, the events of the apocalypse unfold in the present, not in a distant, indeterminate future. Black theology has always hinged on the attempt to make Christianity relevant to day-to-day life in white society. Eschatology, a controversial aspect of Judeo-Christianity, is therefore restructured in light of the struggle for selfhood. The seemingly unchanging situation of oppression demands a rejection of an otherworldly ethos and emphasizes achieving progress now.

The most articulate spokesperson for such a view in this sense has been James Cone, whose insightful discussion of eschatology indicates the character of the black apocalyptic vision:

> The most crucial ingredient of black eschatology was its *historicity*. Even when it was no longer feasible to expect radical historical evidence of God's liberation of the oppressed, black slaves' concept of God's future righteousness was always related to their present existence on earth. Eschatology then was primarily a theological perspective on the present which enabled oppressed blacks to realize that their existence transcended historical limitations. This emphasis is, perhaps, the most important contribution of black religion as reflected in the spirituals.[6]

Wilson Jeremiah Moses and David Howard-Pitney suggest that both the belief in a Messianic figure who will liberate the oppressed masses and the rhetoric of the jeremiad have deep roots in black culture.[7] While white Americans espoused a theological perspective which entailed a belief in a futuristic heaven divorced from the present, blacks looked forward to a reversal of their sociopolitical situation in this world and the release that comes from defining the self through terms drawn from within the culture.

Another form of expression revealing of this theological perspective is the sermon, influencing much of African-American writing. In writing his nineteenth-century *Appeal to the Colored Citizens of the World, but in particular, and very expressly, to those of the United States of America*, David Walker owed much to this form. He considers slavery as an example of both the hypocrisy of a bible-believing South and the failure of the ideals set forth in the Declaration of Independence. Much like an Old Testament prophet, Walker calls an apostate America to repentance. Yet the destruction Walker envisions is secular in nature and will occasion the end of a society that is white. Blacks are to act as agents of God's retributive justice upon the slaveholding South. Walker thus plays upon white fears of slave insurrections, and by drawing upon Scripture he helps to recreate among oppressed blacks the national consciousness slavery was to destroy.

Contemporary writer Imamu Amiri Baraka (LeRoi Jones) relies upon the rhetoric of apocalypse in crafting his creative works and expository prose. In writing his essay "The Last Days of the American Empire (including some instructions for black people)," he is a keen social critic surveying aspects of the American scene during the late 1960s and 1970s. He sees in continued inter- and intraracial conflict, global injustice, and urban squalor signs of impending doom and destruction. Because the struggle for a peaceful solution to social, political, and economic problems has yielded only minimal progress, he foresees a violent overthrow of the white power structure. It is the armed revolutionary who will execute justice on such a racist society: "I say if your hope is for the survival of this society, this filthy order, no good. You lose. The hope is that young blacks will remember all of their lives what they are seeing, what they are witness to just by being alive and black in America, and that eventually they will use this knowledge scientifically, and erupt like Mt. Vesuvius to crush in hot lava these willful maniacs who call themselves white Americans" (*Home* 208–9).

The urban migration of the 1920s and 1930s during which blacks traveled *en masse* from the rural South to the urban North in search of increased social, political, and economic opportunities is the historic event that has had the most profound influence on the conceptualization and development of the apocalypse. In its twentieth-century manifestation, the notion of the end of the world is refracted into ideologies that are directed toward resolving complex modern issues in a literate, fast-paced, technological society. In the 1920s, Marcus Garvey offered hope to thousands of blacks through the creation of a nationalist consciousness that centered around the promise of a reclaimed Africa where blacks could establish an independent nation. Although Garvey's colonization scheme was never realized, he succeeded at restoring dignity among those whose sense of self had been destroyed.

Decades later, apocalypse figures in the ideologies of the Civil Rights Movement and the Black Revolution. While freedom marchers under the leadership of Martin Luther King Jr. hoped for a peaceful solution to continued racial repression, those in the Black Revolutionary Movement of the late sixties and early seventies foresaw direct confrontation as perhaps the only means by which sociopolitical progress could be achieved. The tension between these two ideologies shows the poles between accommodation and militancy that have been present throughout history. What is at issue with both are questions regarding the feasibility of violence in the attempt to establish the new world order. Because the government has been slow in fulfilling the promises of democracy, there are those whose revolutionary ideals have prompted them to advocate the use of force as a way of bringing about positive change. D. S. Russell's discussion of the term *apocalypse* as it is used in the modern era is both instructive and relevant:

> It is with reference to violence and the use of violence that the word *apocalyptic* is perhaps most widely (and most loosely) used at this present time. Ours is an era in which violence has erupted, not just in the form of wars and civil wars, but also in the form of civil strife of many and diverse kinds. On the one hand, civil rights movements have sought to follow the line of nonviolence; on the other hand, revolutionary movements have resorted to the persuasion of the gun. "Freedom marchers" and "freedom fighters" have, in more than one country, highlighted the problem with which democracy generally and Christians in particular find themselves faced. It was in such circumstances as these that Jewish apocalyptic sprang to birth and Christian apocalyptic first became evident. The same spirit of despair and hope prevails today and provides conditions in which the same aspirations are expressed by religious and secular writers alike. (20)

Each of the seven novels included in this study is structured around a catastrophe of some sort—either actualized in the text or anticipated. That catastrophe is to bring about an end to an old social order and give way to a new beginning. Charles Chesnutt's second novel, The Marrow of Tradition, a rewriting of the political agitation leading to the historic 1898 Wilmington, North Carolina, riot, culminates in a full-fledged racial clash resulting in the deaths of the obsequious Mammy Jane and the militant Josh Green whose ideologies are hostile to the southern utopia Chesnutt envisions. Likewise, the Harlem riot in Ralph Ellison's Invisible Man represents a clash not just among people, but the various political ideologies posing as solutions to the race problem. The event forces the narrator to retreat into an underground coal cellar. In the case of Richard Wright, although the Armageddon the Communist attorney Boris Max foresees has yet to take place, his impassioned address to a white judge and jury links Bigger's murder of Mary Dalton with an oppressive social, political, and economic system in such a way as to make the projected clash seem an imminent threat. That Gloria Naylor's community of women gather to dismantle the ominous brick wall isolating them from the outside world is a symbolic gesture on their part signaling the collective desire to escape the restrictions of the white male power structure responsible for Brewster's creation.

The order of inclusion of the novels under investigation is chronological, from Chesnutt to Naylor, and a variety of concerns and techniques are represented. Each novel relies upon apocalypse as an idiom, however. Since the dominant mode present throughout is irony, this study directs close attention to the ways the novelist attempts to reverse or subvert the notion of the end of the world present in mainstream America. Underlying Chesnutt's idealized portrait of the New South as Eden or New Jerusalem is the threat of violent upheaval ritualized in the badman hero tale that serves as a subtext for the novel. Bigger Thomas's experiences in an urban promised land, like those of countless other African Americans, point to the limitations of race and class. Toni Morrison suggests Africa, not America, as the source of a renewed sense of self and community for the race. Together, the seven novels under investigation indicate both the richness and variety of the apocalypse as an idiom and shed light on the ongoing and often elusive quest for equality in a peculiarly American promised land.

CHAPTER 1

Charles Chesnutt, *The Marrow of Tradition*

Go down, Moses, 'Way down in
Egypt land, Tell ole Pharaoh,
To let my people go.

Negro Spiritual

In writing his second novel, *The Marrow of Tradition*, Chesnutt fictionalizes the political agitation leading to the historic 1898 Wilmington, North Carolina, race riot, relying heavily upon folkloric accounts detailing the exploits of the badman hero. Josh Green emerges during the novel's climactic scene as a heroic figure whose vendetta against powerful whites signals the failure of the New South to usher in an era of racial harmony and cooperation. Nevertheless, Chesnutt's optimism concerning the possibilities for positive social and political change prompts his moderate race stance. He moves away from the apocalyptic end that the riot implies and presents an idealistic portrait of life in the region.

Fictionalizing the Badman Hero Tale

Charles Chesnutt's *The Marrow of Tradition*, one of the earliest apocalyptic novels in the African-American tradition, is a careful rewriting of the political tensions leading to the 1898 Wilmington race riot. That the author turns attention to the folklore of the region he knew so well in crafting the novel is not surprising. It was his skill at subjecting this material to the requisites of fictional discourse that brought him wide critical acclaim with the publication of *The Conjure Woman*. The venerable Uncle Julius McAdoo is a wily former slave grounded in the storytelling tradition important to the life and culture of the rural South. As he weaves his stories of magic, superstition, and mysticism for a white northern businessman and his wife, he becomes a living repository of local legend, a gifted teller of tales adept at recreating a past that was becoming increasingly more remote. Chesnutt's second novel is erected on this same folkloric foundation. He makes use of a narrative convention present in local-color writing when he employs Mammy Jane Letlow's voice as a means of offering insight into the history underlying the ongoing conflict between the Carterets and Millers: "Julia had a easy time; she had a black gal ter wait on her, a buggy to ride in, an' eve'ything she wanted. Eve'ybody s'posed Mars Sam would give her a house an' lot, er leave her somethin' in his will. But he died suddenly, and didn' leave no will, an' Mis' Polly got herse'f 'pinted gyardeen ter young Mis' 'Livy, an' driv Julia an' her young un out er de house, an' lived here in dis house wid Mis' 'Livy till Mis' 'Livy ma'ied Majah Carteret."[1]

Interwoven into the narrative structure, as an interesting sideline to the story of familial strife, is the fortune of the Carterets' only child, Theodore Felix, whose life hangs in the balance on a number of occasions: with his premature birth, when he accidentally swallows part of a rattle, and when he is sick with the croup. Jane sees in the small mole behind the child's left ear a sign of possible tragedy, and her sensibilities, like those of many African slaves in the New World, allow her to reconcile a belief in Christianity with the power of conjure. She not only prays for the child's welfare but visits the local conjure woman in search of a good-luck charm to ward off the misfortune to which Theodore Felix seems destined.

As a member of the younger generation, the child is a guardian of the future. In Jane's world view, the future is determined as much by the supernatural as by the sociopolitical forces in Wellington. Jane unearths the good-luck charm the conjure woman gives her after first burying it in the backyard, shakes the bottle vigorously, and then reburies it. As a means of safeguarding the potency of the potion, she makes the sign of a cross over the burial space and walks around it three times. Religion and conjure, sacred and profane coalesce in Jane's mind and lend a richness and depth to narrative action.

There is one aspect of the folk tradition in particular that sparks Chesnutt's artistic imagination in the writing of this text: the account of the badman folk hero whose presence signals an end to white rule. Descriptions of local brawler Josh Green as "a black giant" with "a reputation for absolute fearlessness" recall tales involving the exploits of legendary figures like Jesse James, Billy the Kid, even the biblical Moses, or the notorious lawbreaker Stagolee (109). As H. Nigel Thomas observes, it is Charles Chesnutt who, along with Paul Laurence Dunbar, started the tradition of making use of figures from folklore as major characters in fiction (88). Green attains heroic stature during the novel's fictive apocalypse, figured by the Wellington riot. Not only does Chesnutt engage his audience's attention by creating such a character, on a subliminal level the author manipulates white fears concerning the actions of one who, by his willful disregard for authority, poses a very real threat to a reactionary southern power structure.

Little is known of Green's background or history, except through his childhood recollections of the death of his father at the hands of the Ku Klux Klan and the resulting psychological trauma Green's mother experienced. His memories of his father's murder direct attention to the kind of life-threatening violence to which African-American men in the region were often subject. The African-American man who dared to assert his masculinity placed himself at risk for a quick reprisal from whites, frequently in the form of lynching. Carteret and his fellow politicians are more than willing to resort to the practice as a way of punishing Sandy for the murder of Polly Ochiltree. The suggestion of a possible rape in addition to the murder allows them to play upon white fears regarding the sexual prowess of the African-American male. Sandy, though innocent of the crimes, is to be held as an example to others of what happens to one who "laid sacrilegious hands upon white womanhood" (186). Debate over the use of lynching as a means of social control is centralized in the news media, and Chesnutt maintains a large degree of fidelity to historic events in his account of the efforts on the part of the white power structure to intimidate black voters.[2]

This repressive environment nurtures Green. His tendency toward violent confrontation, his bravado, his utter fearlessness, even in the face of possible death, make him a character ripe for conflict. Addison Gayle Jr. puts it another way: "Men like Green, potential anarchists, are warnings of the Gotterdammerung to come if no modus vivendi can be worked out between the Adam Millers and the Major Carterets" (The Way of the New World 64–65). Green carries bitterness rooted in a past that was "branded on my mem'ry, suh, like a red-hot iron bran's de skin" (111). Because of his quick temper, he finds himself in numerous confrontations. Each of them, as far as he is concerned, is just dress rehearsal for his engagement with McBane, the man directly responsible for the breakup of Green's family.

Wellington's power structure hinders any attempts Green might make toward moving forward to assume a place in the New South. Their vision of the future is one in which aristocratic whites maintain sovereignty. The trio consisting of Carteret, Belmont, and McBane represent the kind of corrupt political alliances in existence at the turn of the century. Green's enemy McBane, formerly a member of the poor white class, is a social climber who amasses a fortune from questionable dealings as a holder of a contract with the state for its convict labor. By virtue of his entry into the political arena, he helps to reinforce the utter powerlessness Wellington blacks experience. Gayle's comments on the antagonism between Green and McBane suggest the volatile nature of their relationship: "Green and McBane represent the forces of irreconcilation pronounced in the town of Wellington. Centuries of antagonism between Blacks and Whites have resulted in a vendetta between the two. This vendetta is the marrow of tradition, and if tradition continues unchanged, the smoldering fires of mistrust, hatred, and discontent will explode in conflagration marked by violence" (*The Way of the New World* 65). The riot taking place in Wellington is then the inevitable outcome of racial tensions that have long been building. It is a statement of the South's failure to bring about a peaceful coexistence between the races.

Chesnutt gives careful attention to the role the news media plays in perpetuating race antagonism. Racial stereotypes abound in *The Morning Chronicle*. Revelations that the paper is "the leading organ of [Carteret's] party and the most influential paper in the State" direct attention to the way the news media can reinforce prevailing social attitudes (2). Nowhere is this more apparent than in Carteret's race-baiting editorials written in response to Sandy's alleged murder and rape of Polly Ochiltree. Carteret casts Sandy in the role of the oversexed black brute obsessed with white women. The comparatively slight attention the paper devotes to news of Sandy's innocence offers a strong indictment of the biased reportage of a conservative media. New, aggressive leadership is needed if the paper is to assume a positive role in promoting sociopolitical change in the New South. Chesnutt is cautious about the possibility of this kind of change, however. When, at the height of the riot, apprentice editor Lee Ellis has an opportunity to speak out against the actions of the white mob, he chooses to remain silent. Responsibility for altering the media's role in the future therefore rests squarely on the shoulders of young Theodore Felix, sole heir to the Carteret estate.

Chesnutt's message of race equality is intended to demythologize white lore encoded in the public sphere. As far as he is concerned, the apocalypse is to occasion a radical change in the social order—one which limits the achievements of aspiring African Americans. His technique is to present black characters whose accomplishments and exemplary behavior signal the progress the race has made since slavery. A member of the talented tenth, Chesnutt felt that only the best among the races were to assume leadership positions in the coming new world order and his black characters have ideologies that either affirm or challenge his progressive outlook. Mammy Jane, her grandson Jerry, and Delamere's servant Sandy are mere types whose presence is designed to appeal to the popular demand on the part of a predominantly white reader-audience for racial stereotyping. The servants are holdovers from the Plantation School, acceptable only in menial roles that do not pose a threat to white rule. Carteret espouses the bigoted race stance that has delimited their achievement. The servants remain content with their places in the southern hierarchy and are distinguished by a syrupy dependence upon their white patrons.

However, Green chooses to reject the limiting roles white society would assign to him, and in moving beyond the servile complacency of Mammy Jane Letlow, he assumes a more militant posture related to the collective desire for freedom on the part of the black masses who, like Janet Miller, are dispossessed. The role, legitimized by rural black southern culture, of the badman hero proves to be especially appealing. This role allows him (and Chesnutt) space to challenge those time-honored notions of white supremacy central to Old South society. Armed with his acute sensitivity to the injustices white society inflicts upon the African-American male, he is constantly at odds with Wellington's reactionary power structure. "The Bad Nigger of folklore is tough and violent," Daryl Dance observes. "He kills without blinking an eye. He courts death constantly and doesn't fear dying, probably because he is willing to do battle with the Devil as well as with his human enemies (and he frequently defeats even the Devil). He values fine clothes and flashy cars. He asserts his manhood through his physical destruction of men and through his sexual victimization of women."[3] Dance's assertions offer a convenient springboard for a more in-depth exploration of Chesnutt's fictionalization of accounts involving the exploits of the badman hero. Green is indeed a daring figure, unafraid of either violent confrontation or death. He tells Miller after one of many brawls, "I expec's ter die a vi'lent death in a quarrel wid a w'ite man . . . an' fu'thermo,' he's gwine ter die at the same time, er a little befo'" (110). The rural setting in which Green comes of age is one where violence is a constant reality. The many deaths that occur during the riot are a reminder of this bitter truth. Even the Millers lose their only son as a result of the clash.

Contrary to what Dance and H. C. Brearly suggest regarding the motives underlying the acts of the badman hero, however, Green's assertion of manhood does not depend upon his sexual exploits with women; his immediate goal is vengeance, not feminine approval.[4] Chesnutt skirts the sensitive issue of black male sexuality altogether with his characterization of the ostensibly single and celibate Josh Green, whom the reader sees only in the broad contexts of work, community leadership, and confrontation. Green's mother, Aunt Milly, is the sole female with whom he is closely associated—and she never makes an appearance in the text. The servants Sandy and Jerry are asexual figures lacking in the qualities essential to genuine manhood. Their dependence upon the goodwill of powerful, monied whites has resulted in a figurative emasculation nearly as devastating as the castration whites often inflicted upon the African-American male who failed to realize his place. Only with Chesnutt's representation of the relationship between Miller and wife Janet is there a hint of the presence of a sexually alive African-American male, and even then, the progeny of that marital relationship—the Miller's only son—remains nameless and is a casualty of the riot. Whatever sexual prowess is attributed to the African-American male exists only the imaginations of the rural white South, or as Chesnutt reveals, in Carteret's incendiary editorials in The Morning Chronicle.

Green's race places him at odds with what Brearly describes as the classic badman hero. According to Brearly, "The person of mixed blood, it is generally believed, is more likely than the black to attempt the part of the 'bad' Negro. This is probably true, for the average mulatto feels superior to blacks and often welcomes a chance to demonstrate his importance" (585). Chesnutt dispels the myth suggesting that persons of mixed race are somehow predisposed to violence. Both Miller and wife Janet are mulattoes, and Janet, Chesnutt informs the reader, "was of a forgiving temper; she could never bear malice" (66). Green, by contrast, who has a violent temper, is not of mixed race.

Moreover, Green enjoys a oneness with the working class, unlike the upper-middle-class, college-educated Miller. Miller reveals the tremendous psychological gulf separating him from the rural folk among whom he lives and works when he is forced to ride in a Jim Crow train. "They were noisy, loquacious, happy, dirty, and malodorous," he observes regarding those who help perpetuate the culture which spawns Green. "For a while Miller was amused and pleased. They were his people, and he felt a certain expansive warmth toward them in spite of their obvious shortcomings. By and by, however, the air became too close, and he went out upon the platform" (60–61).

Whereas Miller remains at a distance from the folk, Green is thoroughly united with them. His confrontations occur, for the most part, among those outside of the race.[5] The incident involving his run-in with a South American, evidently a brawler in his own right, allows Green to make use of the bravado so often a hallmark with the badman hero. Green is quick to respond to Miller's inquiry about the physical condition of the South American: "Lemme see," said Josh reflectively, "ef I kin 'member w'at did become er him! Oh, yes, I 'member now! Dey tuck him ter de Marine Horspittle in de amberlance, 'cause his leg wuz broke, an' I reckon somethin' must 'a' accident'ly hit 'im in de jaw, fer he wuz scatt'rin' teeth all de way 'long de street. I didn' wan' ter kill de man, fer he might have somebody dependin' on 'im, an' I knows how dat 'd be ter dem. But no man kill call me a damn' low-down nigger and keep on enjoyin' good health right along" (109–10). During the riot Green demonstrates his unity with the black masses, mobilizing them into action against the white mob.

Chesnutt's fictional account of the confrontation between Green and McBane lends itself well to a comparison with folkloric representations of the exploits of Stackolee. In one version of the story, the hero, who is armed with a sawed-off shotgun and a deck of cards, has a run-in with the local bartender. A disagreement between the two prompts Stackolee to shoot his opponents. The sharp-tongued, gun-toting, card-playing lawbreaker is no match for them. After killing them he chooses to ritualize his badness in verse: "I was born in the backwoods, for my pet my father raised a bear. / I got two sets of jawbone teeth, and an extra layer of hair. / When I was three I sat in a barrel of knives. / A rattlesnake bit me and crawled off and died" (Abrahams 240).

Still another version of the popular tale pits Stagolee against the new sheriff in a small town in Georgia. The former sheriff is killed when he tries to arrest Stagolee for violating the town ordinance prohibiting drinking after midnight. His successor, determined to bring the hero to justice and therefore restore law and order, waits until Stagolee is sleeping off the effects of a drunken binge before arriving. The results of his attempts to lynch Stagolee are laced with humor:

> After the sheriff had assured them that Stagolee was so drunk he couldn't wake up, they broke in the house just as bad as you please. They had the lynching rope all ready, and they dropped it around his neck. The minute that rope touched Stack's neck, he was wide awake and stone cold sober. When white folks saw that, they were falling over each other getting out of there. But Stack was cool. He should've been. He invented it.
> "Y'all come to hang me?"

The sheriff said that that was so. Stagolee stood up, stretched, yawned, and scratched himself a couple of times. "Well, since I can't seem to get no sleep, let's go and get this thing over with so I can get on back to bed."

They took him on out behind the jail where the gallows was built. Stagolee got up on the scaffold, and the sheriff dropped the rope around his neck and tightened it. Then the hangman opened up on the trap door, and there was Stack, swinging ten feet in the air, laughing as loud as you ever heard anybody laugh. They let him hang there for a half-hour, and Stagolee was still laughing.

"Hey, man! This rope is ticklish."

The white folks looked at each other and realized that Stack's neck just wouldn't crack. So they cut him down, and Stagolee went back home and went back to bed.

After that, the new sheriff left Stagolee in peace, like he should've done to begin with. (Lester 80–81)

Eventually, Stagolee dies. He arrives later in heaven but feels out of place in the presence of its orderliness and tranquillity. His tale closes with his decision to leave heaven and "rule Hell by myself!" (Lester 90).

Perhaps more than any other version of the badman hero tale, it is the story of Morris Slater, better known as Railroad Bill, that likely served to inspire Chesnutt in his creation of Josh Green. Slater, a big, dark-brown man from Alabama, acquires the name Railroad Bill because he hopped onto freight trains in order to make his getaways and robbed trains so that he could make a living. According to local legend, Slater would throw canned goods off of a moving train, return later to the site, and then either eat the food or sell it to the folk cheaper than white storekeepers could sell the same thing. One day a white policeman tries to take away the hunting rifle Slater carries. Slater shoots the policeman and then runs away. Attempts to capture Slater are repeatedly frustrated:

A freight train happened to be racketing past the town at the moment, so Slater hopped it to get away. Bands of men hunted for him all through the area, but they never found him. It was after this first escape that people began to call him Railroad Bill. Slater rode the freight until he came to a thickly wooded region far from town. Then he jumped off and lit into the woods. He found an old voodoo man back there and lived with him a long time. He would help the old fellow—get his firewood or go hunting and bring home meat—and in return the old man taught him some of his voodoo secrets and powers.

After that it seemed as if Railroad Bill had luck with everything, robbing stores and trains. He always got his man and no man ever got him. Year after year the posses hunted him, sometimes with dogs, but never caught him. (Leach 175–76)

As an outlaw who makes use of conjure and defies law and order, Railroad Bill is welcomed among the folk. One day he is caught and killed. But the folk who look to him as a demigod immortalize him through story and song: "Railroad Bill! Dead? Not him!" (Leach 176).

Chesnutt adheres closely to the basic structure of the badman hero account, adding little in the way of narrative embellishments in the transition from folklore to fiction. Green first appears after stealing a ride to Wellington on the trucks of a passenger car. From then until the time of his confrontation with McBane, his life is directed toward righting past wrongs. It is he who assumes leadership of the masses when Miller and Attorney Watson refuse.

Green, on the other hand, "with the eye of a general," like Moses in defiance of Egypt's repressive Pharaoh, mobilizes the masses to action (299). As far as he is concerned, force is the only effective means of dealing with racist opposition. Green's declaration that he would "ruther be a dead nigger any day dan a live dog" stems from his firm adherence to an ethic of violence at odds with Miller's pacifism (284).

It is with a dogged determination to right the wrongs of the past that Green confronts McBane. Even though he has no chance of succeeding as the heavily armed whites surround the burning hospital where Green and other rioting blacks have taken refuge, he remains courageous. Green's bravery in the midst of certain defeat inspires the other rioting blacks to charge the angry white mob. One cannot help but discern Chesnutt's obvious admiration for Green who no doubt becomes a legendary figure among Wellington blacks as a result of his bravery. Green avenges the death of his father by stabbing McBane. He then dies "with a smile still upon his face" (309).

Although Chesnutt holds a certain admiration for Green, he is nonetheless critical of the use of violence as a means of redressing racial injustice. Miller's racial stance is thus not only the more tenable of the two positions the author explores, it is the only one on which any lasting peace in the New South can be achieved. In the novel's closing scenes, Miller, the epitome of black middle-class success, emerges from the post-apocalyptic wreckage and is en route to the Carteret mansion where he is to save the life of Theodore Felix.

By making use of the group experiences of African Americans, Chesnutt calls into question the notion that racial antagonisms ended with Emancipation. But his faith in white society led him to abandon his potentially militant stance. It is not Green but Miller who survives the apocalypse. Chesnutt was not so naive as to believe that change could occur overnight, however. It took decades to spawn the gulf separating the races, and it would take much time to resolve those problems. "Sins, like snakes, die hard," the author interjects early in the text. "The habits and customs of a people were not be changed in a day, nor by the stroke of a pen" (7). Even so, *The Marrow of Tradition* goes against the grain of nationalism that characterizes the black literary apocalypse and presents a portrait of a New South characterized by harmony and cooperation between the best of both races.

Washingtonian Idealism Revisited

The apocalyptic riot taking place in Wellington is a culminating event that sheds light on the tensions between Chesnutt's race stance and that of Booker T. Washington, whose rise to a position of prominence in the realm of national politics paralleled the stripping away of virtually every vestige of black civil and political rights.[6] Chesnutt felt that Washington had rendered a disservice to the majority of African Americans. What Washington chose to emphasize was industrial education, the acquisition of wealth, and accommodation. Chesnutt, on the other hand, valued higher education, full civil and political rights, and he did not hesitate to level criticism at a white southern power structure.

It is, of course, in his controversial "Atlanta Exposition Address" that Washington outlines his philosophy. In response to white patronage he promises black cooperation with the social system. "In all things that are purely social we can be as separate as the fingers," Washington proclaims. "Yet one as the hand in all things essential to mutual progress" (157). Washington concludes his address with a utopian image of the New South:

> In conclusion, may I repeat that nothing in thirty years has given us more hope and encouragement, and drawn us so near to you of the white race, as this opportunity offered by the Exposition; and here bending, as it were, over the altar that represents the results of the struggles of your race and mine, both starting practically empty-handed three decades ago. I pledge that in your effort to work out the great and intricate problem which God has laid at the doors of the South, you shall have at all times the patient, sympathetic help of my race; only let this be constantly in mind, that, while

from representations in these buildings of the product of field, of forest, of mine, of factory, letters, and art, much good will come, yet far above and beyond material benefits will be that higher good, that, let us pray God, will come, in a blotting out of sectional differences and racial animosities and suspicions, in a determination to administer absolute justice, in a willing obedience among all classes to the mandates of law. This, then, coupled with our material prosperity, will bring into our beloved South a new heaven and a new earth. (158–59)

What Washington describes is an Eden characterized by a peaceful coexistence among the races, and he uses glowing terms recalling John the Revelator's vision of a new heaven and earth. Washington's Eden is a uniquely southern and industrialized one, however, emerging as a result of the careful accumulation of wealth. All African Americans need to do in order to gain entry into this earthly paradise is practice the virtues of patience, industry, and thrift. In time, they would become important contributors to the southern economy.

Chesnutt deconstructs Washington's utopian image of the New South, challenging not only the leader's ideals, but those of nineteenth-century America as well. The servants Mammy Jane, Sandy, and Jerry play a self-effacing role in dealing with powerful whites, but are not rewarded for their efforts. Jane's comments to Carteret are patently Washingtonian:[7] "I's fetch' my gran'son' Jerry up ter be 'umble, an' keep in 'is place. An' I tells dese other niggers dat ef dey'd do de same, an' not crowd de w'ite folks, dey'd git ernuff ter eat, an' live out deir days in peace an' comfo't" (43–44). Carteret bestows questionable commendations upon Jerry: "Jerry, now, is a very good negro. He's not one of your new negroes, who think themselves as good as white men, and want to run the government. Jerry knows his place,—he is respectful, humble, obedient, and content with the face and place assigned to him by nature" (87). And Delamere's servant Sandy, a comical figure both in manner and dress, is just as class-conscious as are Wellington's aristocratic whites. The deaths of Mammy Jane and Sandy are thus framed within the context of the failure on the part of whites to protect black citizens. The two are victims of mob violence—and they are killed while in search of their patrons. Chesnutt leaves no room for question regarding his attitude toward Mammy Jane's dated ideals.

It is largely through the characterization of Miller and his wife Janet that Chesnutt challenges Washingtonian idealism. Miller is the offspring of industrious stock. His grandfather, an ex-slave, buys his freedom and passes on to his son Adam a belief in the Protestant Work Ethic. A stevedore by trade, Adam makes a living by working with his hands, hoping that one day "his children or his grandchildren might be gentlemen in the town where their ancestors had once been slaves" (50). While Adam Miller's oldest son follows in his father's footsteps by becoming a stevedore, William Miller breaks with that tradition in pursuit of a medical career.

Chesnutt emphasizes that mulattoes Miller and his wife are just like whites. Miller has reached a level of physical and moral excellence rivalling that of his teacher, Dr. Burns. Chesnutt's creation of the Millers is consistent with his reformist purposes in writing. He mentions his intentions in a journal entry:

> Besides, if I do write, I shall write for a purpose, a high, holy purpose, and this will inspire me to greater effort. The object of my writings would be not so much the elevation of the colored people as the elevation of the whites— for I consider the unjust spirit of caste which is so insidious as to pervade a whole nation, and so powerful as to subject a whole race and all connected with it to scorn and social ostracism—I consider this a barrier to the moral progress of the American people; and I would be one of the first to head a determined, organized crusade against it. Not a fierce indiscriminate onset, not an appeal to force, for this is something that force can but slightly affect, but a moral revolution which must be brought about in a different manner. The subtle almost indefinable feeling of repulsion toward the Negro, which is common to most Americans—cannot be stormed and taken by assault; the garrison will not capitulate, so their position must be mined, and we will find ourselves in their midst before they think it.
>
> This work is of a twofold character. The Negro's part is to prepare himself for recognition and equality, and it is the province of literature to open the way for him to get it—to accustom the public mind to the idea; to lead people out, imperceptibly, unconsciously, step by step, to the desired state of feeling. If I can do anything to further this work, and can see any likelihood of obtaining success in it, I would gladly devote my life to it. (H. M. Chesnutt 21)

Like Washington, Chesnutt believed that African-American progress could occur in the white South, but it would happen largely through efforts on the part of blacks to attain middle-class status. Literature was to be the medium that would allow a predominantly white audience to see images of blacks whose sensibilities were similar to those of whites.

Miller and his wife are models of black achievement, then, and they have risen above the degradation brought about as a result of slavery and caste distinctions. Socially, economically, and politically, Wellington, a microcosm of the South, is on the brink of new beginnings. The generational rift between Mammy Jane, a member of the old guard, and a college-trained nurse reveals the transition the region is undergoing. The most tangible sign of black progress is Miller's hospital, founded with part of his inheritance. It is this building, though, "the fruit of old Adam Miller's industry, the monument of his son's philanthropy, a promise of good things for the future of the city," that fails to offer Josh Green refuge from the rioting white mob (310).

Chesnutt allows the reader a glimpse of the New South with his portrait of the reconciliation between the Millers and Carterets at the novel's post-apocalyptic end. Miller loses his only son in the riot and is at last en route to the Carteret mansion where he is to save the life of Theodore Felix. Social ascent is his goal. Having forsaken the path of vengeance and hatred dictated by history, he becomes a Messianic figure drawn from the middle-class whose presence signals new beginnings. The novel's closing lines convey the sense of urgency out of which Chesnutt writes: "Come on up, Dr. Miller. . . . There's time enough, but none to spare" (329).

Thus, although Chesnutt envisions the apocalypse as being a real threat, the event need not occur. His purpose in writing is social reform, not revolution. Indeed, Sutton Griggs had published a more searing apocalyptic novel, *Imperium in Imperio*, in 1899. Unlike Griggs, Chesnutt hoped that his predominantly white reader-audience would respond more readily to the reasoned plea on the part of the black middle class for social acceptance and then work toward achieving racial harmony. That the twentieth century failed to usher in the new world order Chesnutt foresaw attests to America's resistance to sociopolitical change. His reformist message fell on deaf ears.[8] Nevertheless, the novel is a pioneering work of fiction engaging important issues regarding race, class, and culture to which later writers would return.

CHAPTER **2**   Richard Wright, *Native Son*

> *Let a new earth rise. Let another world be born. Let a bloody peace be written in the sky. Let a second generation full of courage issue forth, let a people loving freedom come to growth, let a beauty full of healing and a strength of final clenching be the pulsing in our spirits and our blood. Let the martial songs be written, let the dirges disappear. Let a race of men now rise and take control!*
>
> Margaret Walker, "For My People"

Native Son is structured around a major catastrophe: the destruction of America. The event is prefigured by Bigger Thomas's murder of Mary Dalton. Attorney Boris Max associates Bigger's act with the impending end of the world, using language suggestive of a coming civil war. The war Max foresees will occur along race and class lines and is to give way to an era of freedom for those once oppressed within a capitalist system. Because America has allowed individuals like Bigger few opportunities for achievement, violence becomes the means by which selfhood is attained.

Racial Armageddon

Richard Wright envisions the apocalypse in secular terms, involving a full-fledged race and class war that will bring an end to America's capitalist system. In a society with an inequitable distribution of wealth the masses, after realizing their revolutionary potential, will rise up and overthrow the ruling class. Bigger Thomas's murder of Mary Dalton foreshadows the larger strife present in America's future. At once both accidental and deliberate, that murder is the catalyst for Bigger's newfound sense of self. He moves outside of society's institutions and achieves freedom through acts of aggression.

Wright would have the reader believe that the seeds of Bigger's defiance exist long before the youth smothers Mary. Max tries in vain to make this point during his impassioned courtroom address. Bigger is America's product, its native son, and his violent tendencies are a direct consequence of the social, economic, and political influences in the larger society. In creating Bigger, what Wright had in mind was a character who would function on a symbolic level, representing the instability of modern America. "Just as one sees when one walks into a medical research laboratory jars of alcohol containing abnormally large or distorted portions of the human body, just so did I see and feel that the conditions of life under which Negroes are forced to live in America contain the embryonic emotional prefigurations of how a large part of the body politic would react under stress."[1] The stress Bigger experiences leads not just to murder, but to a series of challenges directed toward law and order.

In the fictional world Wright constructs, society is divided along race and class lines. It is the Daltons, figures for the ruling class, who are responsible for the harsh ghetto conditions in which Bigger and his family, the urban poor, live. Following in the tradition of the Jeremiad, Max's speech indicts the larger society for its role in perpetuating black exclusion. The Daltons donate millions to black educational institutions. But it is Max who reveals the hypocrisy underlying their philanthropy. Mr. Dalton is manager of South Side Real Estate Company, the company to which Bigger and his family pay rent. By donating money toward furthering the education of African Americans, on the one hand, while extracting an exorbitant rent from the Thomas family, on the other, the Daltons merely contribute to the poverty and social isolation Bigger and his family face.

This is what Max means when he tells Mrs. Dalton, who is literally blind, "Your philanthropy was as tragically blind as your sightless eyes!" (362). Much of Max's speech is directed toward forcing the Daltons into an awareness of their complicity in furthering African-American dispossession. Repeatedly, he pleads for the white judge and jury to "*see* a mode of life in our midst, a mode of life stunted and distorted" (358). Emphasis on sight and blindness are present throughout the novel's tripartite structure.[2] This motif directs attention to the level of political consciousness on the part of modern America. After murdering Mary, Bigger realizes the power he possesses as someone who has stepped outside of the narrow roles that society prescribes for African Americans. No longer is he a mere upholder of America's ideals; instead, at least temporarily, he is a "self-determining" man.

On the morning following Mary's death, Bigger acknowledges the blindness of those around him—that of Mary, Jan, and the members of Bigger's family. Even Bessie Mears is not exempt from the blindness pervasive in

Bigger's world. Because of her commitment to a dead-end job that keeps her confined to a white family's kitchen, Bessie fails to move beyond the narrow orbit into which life has consigned her. The only relief from the monotony of her existence comes through alcohol and sex. It is not surprising that Bigger considers her as being dispensable. After using her as a tool in covering Mary's murder, he kills Bessie. When Bigger rapes Bessie Mears, murders her, then throws her body down an air shaft, he ends a life characterized by aimlessness and despair.

Wright's characterization of Bigger dictates that the protagonist not only discovers the naïveté of those around him, but that he exploits it for personal gain. Detective Britten is at first unaware of Bigger's role in Mary's death. Indeed, the detective considers Bigger as being too ignorant to carry out such a crime. Bigger manages to deceive Britten when engineering the cover-up of Mary's death. Bigger is successful as well at eluding the police after the discovery of Mary's corpse, and Wright makes an important point concerning the role that a politically conscious individual could play in hastening an apocalypse. One man, Bigger Thomas, no longer a passive follower of society's rules and regulations, throws Chicago into a state of chaos.

It is not until Bigger comes to realize the falsity underlying notions of equality that he becomes a threat to the larger society, however. At first he too, like those around him, follows the route to fulfillment that society outlines. Bigger expresses his heroic ideals when he observes an airplane flying overhead. He longs to be a part of the modern world of steel and stone, telling Gus, "I could fly one of them things if I had a chance" (20). Gus's realistic response reminds Bigger of the limitations ghetto life presents: "If you wasn't Black and if you had some money and if they'd let you go to that aviation school, you could fly a plane." Later, as Bigger awaits trial, he tells Max that he wanted to be a pilot, but was not allowed to attend flight school. Bigger therefore fails to fulfill his heroic ideals, represented by the metaphor of flight—a metaphor which, in this context, could be considered a manifestation of a popular motif in African-American folklore suggestive of a return to a mythic past.[3] Unlike his folkloric counterpart who might be able to escape linear time and recover a lost past, Bigger is confined to a movement on ground level. He operates, as Nathan Scott comments, "on a purely horizontal dimension, not the dimension of eternity and the supernatural but the dimension of history and social exclusion" (132). When Bigger accepts the job as chauffeur for the Dalton family, he experiences a sense of empowerment from driving the family's Buick rather than by soaring above the clouds.

Since America's institutions are under the control of whites and the well-to-do, Bigger has few opportunities for advancement. The usual means by which progress occurs are inaccessible as far as he is concerned. Bigger is acutely aware of this dilemma, especially when forced to accept the job as chauffeur. Mrs. Thomas feels that his acceptance of the job will mean an end to the Thomas family's poverty. When she tells Bigger that "we wouldn't have to live in this garbage dump if you had any manhood in you," she equates manhood with economic empowerment (12). Unwittingly, Mrs. Thomas is spokesperson for a system that emasculates African-American men by denying them access to the material rewards signifying manhood. Bigger realizes the falsity underlying his mother's beliefs, however. The relief agency job she urges him to take forces his dependence on an oppressive welfare system. "Yes, he could take the job at the Dalton's and be miserable, or he could refuse it and starve. It maddened him to think he didn't have a wider choice of action" (16).

Yet Wright offers the protagonist a possible avenue of escape from the oppressive systems of modern America. Communism is one alternative to the race and class injustices in Bigger's world, and Wright explores this ideology as narrative action moves toward an apocalyptic finale. The text reveals Wright's shifting attitude toward the party.[4] While communism fosters a collective consciousness among members of the black and white working class in the critically acclaimed Uncle Tom's Children, in Native Son Wright is less certain about the party's effectiveness in addressing the needs of the masses.

Mary Dalton makes a number of awkward attempts to collapse the racial distinctions between herself, Jan, and Bigger, but her actions merely emphasize the gulf separating black and white societies. Immediately after she meets Bigger, Mary insists that he call her by her first name, look her in the eyes while speaking, and sit between herself and Jan as the trio drive to Chicago's South Side. Bigger is confused because of her forward manner. Mary probes into Bigger's past by asking questions that are insensitive and condescending. The supreme insult to Bigger's humanity occurs when Mary asks him to sing a spiritual. From Mary's point of view, Bigger is not a comrade; he is something exotic. He has no identity apart from his racial designation.

Bigger behaves in an obsequious manner while in the Daltons' presence, looking downward and speaking in short sentences. By doing this, he feels that he can remain at a comfortable psychological distance from them. Houston Baker considers Bigger's behavior as having roots in the black folk past (*Long Black Song* 122–41). That behavior represents, Baker asserts, a deliberate attempt to play the subservient role whites expect. In her discussion of the novel's tragic cosmology, Joyce Ann Joyce offers an even more thorough assessment of the relationship between Bigger and his wealthy employers: "While the system of slavery represents the most extreme division of American society into two basic subgroups, racism, its replacement, transforms the discriminatory practices of the eighteenth and nineteenth centuries into the cosmological order of segregation. The essence of *Native Son* is that the social, economic, and political practices of segregation foster demeaning, destructive psychological attitudes that imbue the personalities of both Wright's Black and White characters" (30). Joyce's comments stress the psychosocial and historic dimensions underlying Bigger's relationship with the Daltons. Because of the complex forces separating Bigger from the wealthy family, he knows them from a distance. Similarly, they fail to recognize his humanity. The invisible line separating the protagonist from his employers therefore prevents meaningful interracial interaction.

In *Native Son*, it is the conflict inherent in the relationship between the black world, one of powerlessness, poverty, and exclusion, and the white world, one of wealth and privilege, that suggests the Manichaean tensions leading to an apocalypse. Having grown up the Jim Crow South, Wright was well aware of the gulf that separated the races, and in "The Ethics of Living Jim Crow" he details the various ways in which the color line fostered feelings of frustration among southern blacks. Not only did Wright learn to remain deferential to powerful whites, he came to know the dangers associated with a violation of fixed notions of place. In one of his early stories, "Big Boy Leaves Home," the youthful protagonist finds that once he crosses the invisible boundary separating black and white societies, chaos ensues. It is as if he violates a cosmic law dictating that he not exceed the limits society places upon him. Whites accuse Big Boy of rape, they kill his best friend, and he is forced to flee the region while concealed in the back of a truck.

Another one of Wright's early stories sheds even more light on his apocalyptic vision. In "Fire and Cloud" Reverend Taylor undergoes a symbolic conversion that prompts his rejection of a passive, humble stance and his acceptance of a militant posture, which Communists Hadley and Green encourage. Taylor comes of age as a result of his refusal to remain in the subservient role that the Jim Crow South reserves for African Americans. Once he decides to defy the wishes of whites and organize a march among the masses, he exhibits purpose and resolve. At the story's end, he leads the masses in a demonstration against powerful whites.

Many of the stories in Uncle Tom's Children reveal the influence of the religious discourse of the African-American church on Wright's aesthetics. He uses fire, a biblical symbol for judgment and purification, to suggest Taylor's rite of passage. The first and most obvious association of fire is with the physical pain Taylor endures as a result of his beating at the hands of reactionary whites. Taylor's back feels as if it has been "seared . . . with fire" (165). When he tries to put on his shirt following his beating, his "bruised and mangled flesh flamed, glowed white" (166).

Fire also shows the intensity of Taylor's new collectivist ethos. As the preacher addresses the members of his congregation, "Fire burned him as he talked, and he talked as though trying to escape it" (171). Taylor emphasizes the oneness between himself and the dispossessed of both races: "Sistahs n Brothers, Ah know now! An done seen the sign! Wes gotta git together. Ah know what yo life is! Ah done felt it! Its fire! Its like the fire that burned me las night! Its sufferin! Its hell! Ah cant bear this fire erlone!" (178). The spiritual that Taylor and members of his group sing during the march heightens their group consciousness: "So the sign of the fire by night / N the sign of the cloud by dah / A-hoverin oer / Jus befor / As we journey on our way" (178).

More consistent with its association with judgment, fire indicates impending doom and destruction. After his beating, Taylor speaks prophetically of impending catastrophe: "Some days theys gonna burn! Some days theys gonna burn in Gawd Awmightys fire! How come they make us suffer so?" (167). The story's ending links apocalypse with group freedom while Taylor leads the exultant masses in a scene recalling the exodus of Old Testament Jews from Egyptian captivity: "A baptism of clean joy swept over Taylor. He kept his eyes on the sea of black and white faces. The song swelled louder and vibrated through him. This is the way!, he thought. Gawd ain no lie: He ain no lie! His eyes grew wet with tears, blurring his vision: the sky trembled; the buildings wavered as if about to topple; and the earth shook. . . . He mumbled out loud, exultingly: Freedom belongs t the strong!" (179–80).

Native Son, too, is informed by the religious discourse of the African-American church, although this influence is more subtle in Books One and Two— "Fear" and "Flight"—than it is in Book Three, "Fate." Fire reveals the psychological turmoil that Bigger experiences when confronted with society's imposed limitations. Early in the text he tells Gus about feelings of powerlessness: "Every time I think about it I feel like somebody's poking a red-hot iron down my throat. . . . It's just like living in jail. Half the time I feel like I'm on the outside of the world peeping in through a knot-hole in the fence" (23). Gesturing toward his midsection, he informs Gus that whites live "Right down here in my stomach" (24).

The fire of Bigger's frustration becomes more intense as narrative action progresses. At the prospect of robbing a white storeowner, Bigger feels the "ball of tightness grow larger and heavier in his stomach and chest" (37). Bigger's tension mounts steadily until, once alone with Mary in her bedroom, he is "wrapped in a sheet of blazing terror" (88). His placing of Mary's decapitated body in the Dalton furnace represents the fiery culmination of his search for manhood on the terms white society establishes.

In "How Bigger Was Born," Wright mentions his conscious use of opposing ideas and symbols, thus offering the reader insight into the central tensions in the text. While fire is closely associated with the black world, it is ice or snow that is symbolic of the white world.[5] Bigger feels out of place in the Daltons' neighborhood, "a world of white secrets" (45). Once he arrives at their home, the housekeeper Peggy, whom Bigger sees as "a white face," allows him entrance (46). Mr. Dalton is a "white-haired man" who makes Bigger "conscious of every square inch of skin on his black body" (47). Bigger notices that Mrs. Dalton's "face and hair were completely white" (48). Hours later, when Bigger is alone with Mary in her darkened room, he sees Mrs. Dalton as "a white blur" (84). Finally, as Bigger places Mary's body into a furnace, the Daltons' white cat, whose ominous presence is a constant reminder of the white world, oversees the incident.

The most obvious and persistent symbol for the white world is snow, and its role in determining Bigger's fate reveals the naturalistic dimensions of narrative action. The role that snow plays in Bigger's flight and capture is at times ambiguous. At first the snow helps Bigger to elude the police. Later, when they spray him with water, which quickly turns to ice in the frigid temperatures, the snow aids the police in capturing him. Jan and Mary are the two "looming white mountains" whose treatment of Bigger reminds him of his blackness and heightens his frustration (68). It is only at the novel's end that Bigger attempts to reach out to whites—his attorney Max and Jan.

As Wright would have the reader believe, the fire of Bigger's pent-up frustrations poses a very real threat to the white world. That threat is only a tentative one, though. The authorities not only capture Bigger but plan to execute him as well. Only through collective action can the dispossessed masses therefore achieve positive social, economic, and political change. Before he murders Mary, Bigger envisions a utopia where there is solidarity among the black masses. But his ideal of a unified community moving to challenge white rule is tempered by his awareness of a fragmented urban community. By murdering Mary, Bigger is not the powerful political leader he wishes to emulate; nor is he the bold revolutionary that Mary would have him be. He is instead a solitary rebel whose life culminates in an isolated act of violence.

Max's address is an apocalyptic one that lends historic and sociopolitical significance to Bigger's actions, linking the protagonist's self-realization through violence to that of the once dormant masses. In this context, Paul Seigel is accurate in his reading of the underlying significance of "Fate": "It has been frequently pointed out that in Book III, which is entitled 'Fate,' we see realized the doom of Bigger that has been foreshadowed from the beginning. This is entirely true, of course, but 'Fate' also refers to the doom of the United States, toward which Max sees us, 'like sleepwalkers' (324), proceeding" (Richard Wright 110). In addressing a white audience, Max draws upon circular views of time and history popular during the eighteenth century. Past, present, and future are linked in his discourse. The oppression which those in modern America face is a result of the same system responsible for slavery and caste distinctions. If America believes that it is a covenant nation with a moral obligation to administer justice to all individuals, then it can expect retribution for its wrongs. Max manipulates white fears concerning violence as being divine compensation for race and class inequities: "Your Honor, another civil war in these states is not impossible; and if the misunderstanding of what this boy's life means is an indication of how men of wealth and property are misreading the consciousness of the submerged millions today, one may truly come" (369).

Max views African Americans, a nation that is subjugated within American society, as the unstable foundation upon which this country rests. Bigger's crime, therefore, heralds the Armageddon toward which the country is moving. Invoking an emotionally moving image of secular catastrophe, Max suggests, "Who knows when another 'accident' involving millions of men will happen, an 'accident' that will be the dreadful day of our doom?" (369).

In his journey to self-determination, however, Bigger rejects the Communist pleadings of his zealous attorney as freely as he rejects all other imposed systems of thought. Instead, he assumes personal responsibility for his crimes, telling Max in the closing scene: "I didn't know I was really alive in this world until I felt things hard enough to kill for 'em. . . . It's the truth, Mr. Max. I can say it now, 'cause I'm going to die. I know what I'm saying real good and I know how it sounds. But I'm all right. I feel all right when I look at it that way" (392).

Despite Max's apocalyptic rhetoric, the Armageddon of which he speaks is indefinitely forestalled. Nor does a communist utopia come into existence. The text closes with a portrait of the disgruntled urban poor just outside the social mainstream. The novel is, therefore, not a formula for revolution as much as it is a warning concerning the catastrophe that can be avoided. Like an Old Testament prophet whose pronouncements of doom are delayed, Wright wrote in hopes of averting the widespread secular strife looming in the nation's future.

Manchild in the Promised Land

With its emphasis on impending doom and destruction, Max's courtroom address is an apocalyptic one that unifies the tripartite narrative. It is Max, Wright's spokesperson, who places Bigger's actions within their sociopolitical and historic context. According to the Jewish attorney, history is recursive, not linear, and events are interconnected. Bigger's acts of defiance are, in Max's view, signs of the times. They are a foreshadowing of the larger secular strife in America's future. Max foresees the day when those like Bigger will arise and overthrow the prevailing social order.

Wright allows the reader a sneak preview into what the new world order will be like in "Flight," which chronicles Bigger's ironic journey toward manhood. Rather than finding a sense of self through the usual channels of work, the family, or the church, Bigger is suddenly thrust into manhood through a series of challenges to white society. The Bigger who appears in Book Two is quite different from the one in Book One. The protagonist is at first a passive, fearful youth who spends his time engaged in petty crimes. Usually those crimes are violations against other African Americans. When Bigger and his friends plan to rob Blum, that represents their first real act of aggression against whites. Bigger is much too fearful to carry out the robbery. So he chooses to stage a fight with Gus, whom he perceives as being weak. As someone who is a respondent to the external influences in his ghetto environment, Bigger does little to change either his destiny or that of his family and friends.

In Book Two, however, Bigger moves outside the moral order of the dominant society. No longer a boy, he is a man who is shaped by his own actions, not those of others. Narrative action assumes momentum as Bigger moves toward his goal. He is active in disposing of Mary's corpse, deceiving the arrogant Britten, and then eluding the police. The murder of Mary results in his feelings of security: "He had murdered and created a new life for himself. It was something that was all his own and it was the first time in his life he had had anything that others could not take from him" (101). Once he rejects society's prescribed path to fulfillment, Bigger no longer shares a camaraderie with his friends: "He wanted to know how he would feel if he saw them again. Like a man reborn, he wanted to test and taste each thing now to see how it went; like a man risen up well from a long illness, he felt deep and wayward whims" (106). Bigger feels confident around the Daltons: "For the first time in his life he moved consciously between two sharply defined poles: he was moving away from the threatening penalty of death, from the deathlike times that brought him that tightness and hotness in his chest; and he was moving toward that sense of fullness he had so often but inadequately felt in magazines and movies" (141). And finally, after he rapes and murders Bessie Mears, the last cornerstone in his private dystopia is in place: "He had committed murder twice and had created a new world for himself" (226).

Bigger's attainment of selfhood through violence places him in a long line of individuals in literature and life whose rebellion against white society leads to freedom. When he tells Max that "I want to be happy in this world, not out of it" (329), he articulates a belief system at odds with orthodox Christianity. With Bigger, however, there is a reinterpretation rather than a rejection of Judeo-Christian ideals. Early in the text he hears his mother singing a gospel song: "Life is like a mountain railroad / With an engineer that's brave / We must make the run successful / From the cradle to the grave" (14). Later that same day, he hears her sing again: "Lord, I want to be a Christian, / In my heart, in my heart, / Lord, I want to be a Christian, / In my heart, in my heart" (37). Mrs. Thomas's religion is strictly compensatory and the lyrics she intones offer solace in the face of life's challenges. When she speaks of life's journey as being one from the cradle to the grave, she expresses the existential plight of the urban masses whose only hope is for liberation in heaven.

While eluding the police, Bigger hears singing from a church and longs to be a part of the world about which the congregation sings. But he is also aware of the need for a more immediate solution to the problems the masses face. The song that Bigger hears is "Steal Away," once a cultural code among slaves. But the song's radical meaning suggesting the possibility of escaping oppression and finding new life in an urban promised land has no validity from Bigger's vantage point. The lyrics underscore the hopelessness of the urban masses. When Bigger concludes that "It was dangerous to stay here, but it was also dangerous to go out" (238), he indicates his awareness of the limited options of those in the ghetto.

With its focus on the disillusionment faced by the urban masses, Native Son is a text that reverses the notion of the urban North as a promised land. Much like Cross Damon in The Outsider and Fred Daniels in "The Man Who Lived Underground," Bigger, too, sees society from a black point of view. He acts out the role of a militant Christ figure.[6] As he eludes the police, he longs for "someone [who] had gone before and lived or suffered or died— made it so that it could be understood!" (226). When the authorities capture him they stretch his arms out "as though about to crucify him" (253). And as his family visits him in jail he thinks, "Had he not taken fully upon himself the crime of being black?" (275).

Thus, after witnessing the Klan's burning of a cross, Bigger discards the cross which a Catholic priest offers him. He rejects as well the theological perspective that Reverend Hammond presents: "He had killed within himself the preacher's haunting picture of life even before he had killed Mary; that had been his first murder. . . . To those who wanted to kill him he was not human, not included in that picture of Creation; and that was why he had killed it. To live, he had created a new world for himself, and for that he was to die" (264).

From white society's perspective, by contrast, Bigger is a type of Satan, the arch deceiver. Immediately after Bigger murders Mary, his Satanic character is evident as he carries her corpse to the basement, places her partially in the furnace, and—with "an attitude of prayer" (91) which parodies the prayer Mrs. Dalton utters just moments before in Mary's darkened bedroom—decapitates her. Bigger, who earlier felt ill at ease in the Dalton home, is very much at home with the chaos which the flames of the furnace symbolize and uses the confusion stemming from Mary's disappearance to his own advantage.

Buckley's sensationalized courtroom speech casts Bigger in the role of Satan in the American Eden, and the protagonist's presence signals a temporary overthrow of the moral order. Appealing to his audience's beliefs in white supremacy, Buckley tells them that "[e]very decent white man in America ought to swoon with joy for the opportunity to crush with his heel the woolly head of this black lizard, to keep him from scuttling on his belly farther over the earth and spitting forth the venom of death!" (373). The court summons Bigger before the stern, white-faced, black-robed judge who pronounces the protagonist's fate. As if to indicate the sinister nature of Bigger's character, his case is prefixed 666, the number identifying Revelation's Beast.

That Bigger is to die for his crimes indicates the failure on the part of white society to realize its role in perpetuating black exclusion. It is Buckley's racist propaganda, not Max's apology on Bigger's behalf, that holds sway. But as far as *Native Son* is concerned, Bigger's final declaration of self, "what I killed for, I *am!*" (391–92), is a millennial one in the tradition of the African-American novel. Bigger's declaration signals the arrival of an era in which those once outside the social mainstream will no longer tolerate the injustices of the past. Wright's literary apocalypse is then a mature one relegating the American dream to a bygone era.

CHAPTER **3** Ralph Ellison, Invisible Man

I was thinking of a character who was a master of disguise, of coincidence, this name with its suggestion of inner and outer came to my mind. Later I learned that it was a call used by Harvard students when they prepared to riot, a call to chaos.Which is very interesting, because it is not long after Rinehart appears in my novel that the riot breaks out in Harlem. Rinehart is my name for the personification of chaos. He is also intended to represent America and change. He has lived so long with chaos that he knows how to manipulate it. It is the old theme of The Confidence Man. *He is a figure in a country with no solid past or stable class lines; therefore he is able to move about easily from one to the other.*

Ralph Ellison, *Shadow and Act*

In *Invisible Man*, the apocalypse is a tragicomic event figured by the Harlem race riot. It is the last and greatest in a long line of narrative ruptures revealing the chaos underlying American race relations. Only those who are in touch with their folk identities will survive the catastrophe.The riot forces the narrator into a self-conscious realm where he embraces his blackness. Once outside society, he tells his life's story and offers a unique perspective on turbulent modern America.

Tricksters, Confidence Men, and Antichrists

The world evoked in Ralph Ellison's *Invisible Man* is, as R. W. B. Lewis puts it, "spoiling for catastrophe: a world rank with duplicity and violence, infested by cheats, liars, betrayers, and impostors, all caught up in a continuing and somehow wonderfully exuberant masquerade" (218). In his signification upon the Manichaean tensions between black and white that erupt in apocalyptic conflicts, Ellison explores the adaptive modes of behavior that have allowed individuals to survive, even in the most difficult circumstances. As a living embodiment of the endurance capabilities of the folk, the shape-shifting trickster figure holds important lessons in the narrator's search for visibility and freedom. What the narrator learns is that his world is void of moral values. The unwritten codes of conduct governing race relations in modern America are at best uncertain. Deception is therefore society's characteristic feature. Or as one character says, "it is impossible not to take advantage of the people. . . . The trick is to take advantage of them in their own best interest."[1] As he journeys through different segments of America, the narrator confronts authority figures—skilled impostors in their own right—who have a vested interest in keeping him running in pursuit of his middle-class ideals. The narrator's growth toward maturity parallels his ability to strip away the facades which those authority figures wear.

More than any other figure, it is the ubiquitous Rinehart, master of disguise, whose existence signals the chaos present in American society, and as Ellison is quick to point out, it is Rinehart's appearance that immediately precedes the Harlem riot. Indeed, Ellison has provided the reader with a great deal of insight into his fictive apocalypse. Narrative emphasis is on the unstable interracial relationships that suggest the apocalypse as being the inevitable outcome of history. With *Invisible Man* there is no question that the end of the world is imminent. What is at issue is how one is to respond to the event. Various individuals are intent on manipulating the chaos and confusion of twentieth-century America in hopes of seizing control in the post-apocalyptic new world order. By retreating into an underground coal cellar, the narrator has space to contemplate his relationship to society. Moreover, he is able to draw upon the survival skills that have allowed countless others to endure despite the strictures of racial oppression.

At first, the narrator is psychologically distanced from the strategies that have allowed African Americans to negotiate their way through white society. His grandfather, whom Addison Gayle Jr. rightly labels "a wily slave, expert at displaying obsequiousness in dealing with white folks" (*The Way of the New World* 250), imparts timeless wisdom on black survival: "overcome 'em with yeses, undermine 'em with grins, agree 'em to death and destruction, let 'em swoller you till they vomit or bust wide open" (16). The grandfather's cryptic advice becomes a part of the narrator's racial memory. What the former slave advocates is that the narrator use a mask of meekness as a way of attaining his goals. His advice is at once both liberating and limiting. Not only does it provide the narrator with a means of negotiating his way through America's racial structure, it hinders his attainment of a personal identity. Once he assumes such a mask the narrator finds that his true self is concealed.

Ellison resists applying the term "trickster" with reference to the grandfather's role and prefers instead a formalist reading of the text (*Shadow and Act* 55–56). Nevertheless, an examination of the grandfather within the larger context of the trickster tradition sheds light on the close relationship between the novel and its oral antecedents. *Invisible Man* is a novel whose recurring narrative ruptures—mini apocalypses—are revealing of the aboriginal roots undergirding the stylized narrative.[2] Duplicity is a hallmark of the trickster, and the grandfather uses this behavior deftly in moving through the labyrinthine understructure of America's institutions. What motivates him is the desire to survive in a world that fails to acknowledge his humanity. By agreeing with his adversaries, he allows his conformity to work for him while exploiting the willful blindness of others. Although his strategy does not allow him to wrest power from his opponents, it allows him at least a small amount of freedom from the limitations society imposes.

The narrator's introduction to the realities of southern race relations begins with the battle royal episode and continues throughout his enrollment at a black college. In the battle royal, the narrator and his high school classmates must participate in events which reinforce the region's racial and sexual politics. The youths are herded into a crowded elevator, blindfolded, teased, degraded, and forced to fight each other—all for the amusement of the town's leading white citizens. Afterwards, winners of the conflict, the narrator and Tatlock, must retrieve their rewards, "good hard American cash" (27), in the form of brass pocket tokens on an electrified rug.

Presiding over the event is the narrator's high school superintendent, a shadowy figure who hovers ominously in the background sanctioning the degradation the youths undergo. Not only does the superintendent invite the narrator to attend the event, he rewards him with a calfskin brief case and a scholarship to a black college. Only later does the narrator discover the words on a dream-fantasy scholarship which suggest the futility underlying his search for fulfillment in America: "Keep this Nigger-boy running" (33).

Because the superintendent is motivated by a desire to maintain his privileged position within the southern power structure instead of survival, he is a character who is closely aligned with the confidence man.[3] The superintendent is self-serving and intent on maintaining his dominance over the narrator and the other high school students, even if it means exploiting the unsuspecting youths. That he rewards the narrator by giving him a scholarship in the name of the board of education is a telling commentary on the extent to which the educational system furthers the anonymity of African Americans.

Evidence of the South's racial tensions are readily apparent during the battle royal episode. Ellison refers to the ritualistic undertones of the event: "Take the 'Battle Royal' passage in my novel, where the boys are blindfolded and forced to fight each other for the amusement of the white observers. This is a vital part of behavior pattern in the South, which both Negroes and whites thoughtlessly accept. It is a ritual in the preservation of caste lines, a keeping of taboo to appease the gods and ward off bad luck" (*Shadow and Act* 174). The white citizens who witness the degradation of the youths are bankers, doctors, and lawyers—figures for the middle class. Before participating in the battle royal, the youths must watch a nude blonde dancer with an American flag tattooed on her stomach. Only the white citizens are allowed to touch her. The youths merely watch her sensual gyrations. The nude dancer is, as A. Robert Lee describes, a metaphor for mother America, whose social, political, and economic rewards are reserved for whites and the well-to-do (23).

Ellison's literary apocalypse is one that not only challenges the notion of America as being a raceless, classless Eden, it offers a fictionalization of a historic mode in which there is a cyclic repetition of the injustices which African Americans face. Alluding to the novel's recursive structure, Ellison comments on his intentions in writing:

I began it with a chart of the three-part division. It was a conceptual frame with most of the ideas and some incidents indicated. The three parts represent the narrator's movement from, using Kenneth Burke's terms, purpose to passion to perception. These three major sections are built up of smaller units of three which mark the course of the action and which depend for their development upon what I hoped was a consistent and developing motivation. However, you'll note that the maximum insight on the hero's part isn't reached until the final section. After all, it's a novel about innocence and human error, a struggle through illusion to reality. Each section begins with a sheet of paper; each piece of paper is exchanged for another and contains a definition of his identity, or the social role he is to play as defined for him by others. But all say essentially the same thing, "Keep this nigger boy running." Before he could have some voice in his own destiny he had to discard these old identities and illusions; his enlightenment couldn't come until then. Once he recognizes the hole of darkness into which these papers put him, he has to burn them. That's the plan and the intention; whether I achieved this is something else. (*Shadow and Act* 176–77)

As Ellison's comments suggest, the novel is a conscious telling or retelling of the same story. Each subsequent section of the tripartite narrative echoes the previous one, but with a difference, thereby creating a text whose roots are in forms of black oral expression, not just in the Western literary tradition.[4] A veteran shares some timely advice relevant to the complex ritual substructure underlying the text when he tells the narrator to "learn to look beneath the surface" (151).

The narrator's introduction to the South's racial politics continues with his journey to Trueblood's cabin. Trueblood, who is a sharecropper, singer, and gifted teller of tales, is a "true blood" accepting of his place within the rigidly stratified social system. Situated outside the social mainstream, he learns to use his marginalized position to his own advantage. When he tells his sordid tale of incest to the narrator and Norton, the millionaire, who also had a daughter, swoons as if some dark truth has been revealed. He then offers Trueblood a hundred-dollar bill.

While Norton hides behind a mask of upper-middle-class respectability, Trueblood maintains a measure of selfhood that the millionaire and the college-educated narrator lack. Houston Baker comments on Trueblood's blueslike affirmation of life in a catastrophe-ridden rural South: "In translating his tragedy into the vocabulary and semantics of the blues and, subsequently, into the electrifying expression of his narrative, Trueblood realizes that he is not so changed by catastrophe that he must condemn, mortify, or redefine his essential self. This self . . . is in many ways the obverse of the stable, predictable, puritanical, productive, law-abiding ideal self of the American industrial-capitalist society" (*Blues, Ideology, and Afro-American Literature* 190). Trueblood is an embodiment of Norton's dark side, a visible manifestation of the sin, guilt, and chaos that Norton dares not openly acknowledge.

Ellison strips away the mask that Norton wears in the Golden Day Episode. The American dream which the millionaire espouses has gone awry. Its proponents, Norton and Supercargo, are no longer in control. Instead, a group of anonymous prostitutes and shell-shocked veterans determine the events which take place. The veterans—once doctors, lawyers, and teachers—are alumni of the narrator's college. On their return to their alma mater, they are all mad. The American myth of progress is proven false. For the first time in the text there are veiled references to an apocalypse, and the dialogue between the prostitutes and the veterans is laced with humor:

"It will occur at 5:30," he said, looking straight through me.
"What?"
"The great all-embracing, absolute Armistice, the end of the world!" he said.
Before I could answer, a small plump woman smiled into my face and pulled him away.
"It's your turn, Doc," she said. "Don't let it happen till after me and you done been upstairs. How come I always have to come get you?"
"No, its true," he said. "They wirelessed me from Paris this morning."
"Then, baby, me an' you better hurry. There's lots of money I got to make in here before that thing happens. You hold it back a while, will you?"
She winked at me as she pulled him through the crowd toward the stairs. I elbowed my way nervously toward the bar. (73)

In the madness of the Golden Day, confusion regarding Norton's identity reaches its height. He is associated with a series of legendary figures from the realms of politics, high finance, and religion: Thomas Jefferson, John D. Rockefeller, and the Messiah. But Norton is not a Messianic figure whose monied liberalism will redeem African Americans from the shackles of poverty and ignorance. He is a deceptive Antichrist whose presence serves to incite the revolutionary sensibilities of the masses. The revelation occurring in the Golden Day has to do with Norton's Emersonian idealism. Confusion, not upward mobility, is the end result of his belief in the importance of individualism. The veterans have attempted to find a sense of gratification through their professions but have failed. Their fate thus foreshadows that of the idealistic narrator.

Dr. Bledsoe, a fictional projection of Booker T. Washington, dons a mask of meekness and servility that suits his self-serving purposes of trickery and deceit. A legendary figure who rises from obscurity to a place of prominence by practicing the virtues of patience, thrift, and industry, he at first appears to offer a solution the narrator's invisibility. Homer A. Barbee casts Bledsoe into the role of a Moses or Christ figure who is to lead African Americans into a utopia of racial harmony and cooperation. The narrator's description of Bledsoe, however, places Bledsoe within the trickster tradition. As Bledsoe reprimands the narrator for exposing Trueblood to the seamier underside of black life, the reader learns the extent to which masking has distorted Bledsoe's character. H. Nigel Thomas is correct in observing that in Bledsoe, the trickster tradition is taken too far (98). Bledsoe has sacrificed his identity in his attempt to garner power in the South, and in his encounter with the narrator he reveals the strategy that has allowed him to outwit his white and black adversaries. Bledsoe's motives, like that of the wily confidence man, are selfish, not survivalistic, and he is concerned only about maintaining power, even if it means exploiting those of his own race. Bledsoe tells the narrator, "This is a power set-up, son and I'm at the controls. You think about that. When you buck against me, you're bucking against power, rich white folk's power, the nation's power—which means government power!" (140). That the narrator steals power from the Monopolated Light and Power Company suggests his adoption of Bledsoe's strategies. But Ellison does not intend for Bledsoe to be a character worthy of emulation. He has lost his integrity in the manipulation of others. Bledsoe tells the narrator at one point, "I'll have every Negro in the country hanging on tree limbs by morning if it means staying where I am" (141).

Once the narrator travels north to the mythical promised land, he finds that the survival strategies of the folk offer a release from the ongoing tensions present in his world. His experiences bring him into contact with the various institutions, organizations, and systems of thought posing as solutions to the characteristically twentieth-century problem of invisibility. Only by relying upon his racial memory does he maintain a sense of self in a context that would rob him of that identity. Thus, the doctors at the factory hospital who intend to perform a prefrontal lobotomy on the narrator are unsuccessful at erasing his black consciousness. Not only does he recall aspects of his folk past—namely, Brer Rabbit—he at times assumes the role of the wily rabbit as he tries to outrun his adversaries.[5]

One of those adversaries is Brother Jack, self-styled leader of the Brotherhood. The narrator is attracted to the organization because of its emphasis on pattern, discipline, and order. He feels that the group offers him an opportunity to be "more than a member of a race" (346). But it is only in racial terms that the organization recognizes him. Brother Jack's utopian vision of a raceless, classless society recalls that of the Communist Party, despite Ellison's claim that the Brotherhood is not modeled after that group (*Shadow and Act* 179). What the narrator discovers is that the organization plans to use him and other young African Americans as pawns in the manipulation of the disgruntled Harlemites. This is the truth that young Brotherhood disciple Tod Clifton learns. His peddling of Sambo dolls on the

Harlem streets parodies the role he has played while in the Brotherhood ranks.

Brother Jack, an unscrupulous demagogue, is a dissembler who gives the narrator his final identity, Brother X, and assigns him the role of Brotherhood spokesperson in the Harlem district. In spite of the mask of liberalism Brother Jack wears, his historical vision is a narrow one that prevents him from recognizing racial difference. Spiritually and physically blinded by his social vision, Jack, who the narrator discovers has lost his eye in the line of duty, like the employees at Liberty Paints is engaged in a complex scheme involving a whitewash, which will result in the obscuring of the narrator's diverse racial heritage.

With the introduction of Ras the Exhorter, fierce Brotherhood opponent, Ellison directs attention to the racial polarization that will end in apocalypse. Ras's impassioned speeches are designed to appeal to the frustrated masses and they point out the falsity underlying America's ideals. Ellison, who denies that Ras is based on Marcus Garvey, mentions that he sketched Ras in anger (*Shadow and Act* 181). Nevertheless, much like the charismatic Jamaican-born leader, Ras speaks of the black history as being distinct from that of the larger society and looks forward to a collective return to Mother Africa. His ideology is one that appeals to the dispossessed masses and challenges the validity of the Brotherhood's rigid scientific historicism. At one point Ras lectures the narrator and Clifton:

> I ahm no black educated fool who t'inks everything between black mahn and white mahn can be settled with some blahsted lies in some bloody books written by the white man in the first place. It's three hundred years of black blood to build this white mahn's civilization and wahn't be wiped out in a minute. Blood calls for blood! You remember that. And remember that I am not like you. Ras recognizes the true issues and he is not afraid to be black. Nor is he a traitor for white men. Remember that: I am no black traitor to the black people for the white people. (366–67)

Bliss Proteus Rinehart, for whom the narrator is repeatedly mistaken, is one who defies analysis using the Brotherhood's rigid scientific determinism. Although he never appears in the text, everyone, except the narrator, knows of him—and in a different role. He is "Rine the runner, Rine the gambler, Rine the briber, Rine the lover, and Rinehart the Reverend" who invites the public to join him in the "NEW REVELATION of the OLD TIME

RELIGION" (486–87, 484). Rinehart is the supreme incarnation of the chaos of the age. Ellison sheds light on Rinehart's role in narrative action:

> He is a cunning man who wins the admiration of those who admire skull-duggery and know-how; an American virtuoso of identity who thrives on chaos and swift change; he is greedy, in that his masquerade is motivated by money as well as by the sheer bliss of impersonation; he is god-like, in that he brings new techniques—electric guitars, etc.—to the service of God, and in that there are many men in his image while he is himself unseen; he is phallic in his role of "lover"; as a numbers runner he is a bringer of manna and a worker of miracles, in that he transforms (for winners, of course) pennies into dollars, and thus he feeds (and feeds on) the poor. (*Shadow and Act* 56)

Rinehart is a figure whose presence signals the moral chaos of modern America. Because he has no stable class affiliations and is as comfortable with the Harlem underworld as with a monied, technological society, he is an objectification of the hopes of an otherwise hopeless people. H. Nigel Thomas's reading of the text prompts him to see Rinehart as a projection of the narrator's ego (94). R. W. B. Lewis's reading of Rinehart's role in narrative action is more pointed. He considers Rinehart's presence as a sign of the traditional last loosing of Satan or, of "all hell breaking loose" (218). Indeed, the protean figure, like the biblical Antichrist whose coming, according to Scripture, "is after the working of Satan with all power and signs and lying wonders" (II Thessalonians 2:9), reflects the vast fluidity of modern life and its propensity toward violent conflict and upheaval.

From the point of view of his congregation he is a miracle worker with godlike abilities, but he makes clever use of modern technology and charlatanism in exploiting the blindness of his black and white victims. A new convert is impressed by his introduction of a new kind of electric guitar music in his unconventional church services. And as if to indicate the crass materialism that underlies his mask of spirituality, he generates money for his building fund through the sale of recordings of his *one* inspiring sermon.

Rinehart's purpose within the formal structure of the text is not only to call attention to society's heightening moral decay, it is to offer the narrator a way of escaping his pursuers. Moreover, by donning dark green glasses and adopting Rinehart's tactics within the Brotherhood, the narrator unwittingly acts out the grandfather's cryptic advice. He reaches a new level of awareness, however, when he realizes that by affirming his opponents he has cooperated in furthering his own anonymity.

Race, Words, and the War on Invisibility

If the trickster tactics encoded in a rich oral tradition allow the narrator a timely release from a chaotic, fast-paced society headed toward an apocalypse, then his careful manipulation of words is equally as important in his search for visibility. Ellison covered the events surrounding the historic Harlem race riot while he was a reporter for the *Amsterdam News*. In *Invisible Man*, the apocalypse is filtered through the narrator's consciousness, and the most obvious and persistent symbol for the event appears during the riot with the arrival of Ras the Exhorter turned Ras the Destroyer mounted on a great black horse. Ellison adheres closely to the sequential ordering of events constituting the end of the world. According to the Book of Revelation, the arrival of the black horse is to follow that of the Antichrist and world war. But as Ellison employs a first-person point of view in recounting the event, the apocalypse is transformed into a celebration.

While in a drug-induced dream, the narrator hears a singer of spirituals who defines freedom in terms of creative self-expression. Freedom, as the unlettered slave envisions it, "ain't nothing but knowing how to say what I got up in my head" (11). The narrator, who views himself as a future Booker T. Washington, is a gifted orator who hopes to use his oratorical skills in furthering his middle-class aspirations. He admires Frederick Douglass, whose rise from slavery to a position of prominence in national politics has much to do with his facility with language. Brother Tarp gives the narrator a portrait of Douglass, prompting the narrator's realization that there was "a magic in spoken words" (372).

The narrator has an opportunity to test his oratorical skills when he delivers his valedictory address on humility as being the essence of progress in the New South, but the climate of hostility present as the narrator speaks contradicts his Washingtonian ideals. As he gulps blood following the battle royal, the narrator repeats Washington's "Atlanta Exposition Address." When he utters the phrase "social equality" instead of the less threatening "social responsibility," he draws a rather ominous silence from his otherwise inattentive white audience. Almost instinctively, his reactionary auditors remind him of his place.

Ellison's literary apocalypse is one that reveals the realities of life in a racially polarized world. The narrator follows the formula for success that

Washington outlines only to be forced outside of time and history. His naive belief in "the rightness of things" or the democratic principles upon which America was founded, prove deceptive (30). From his enlightened position in the section of a Harlem basement forgotten during the nineteenth century he cautions the reader against an overly simplistic view of historical events: "(Beware of those who speak of the spiral of history; they are preparing a boomerang. Keep a steel helmet handy.) I know; I have been boomeranged across my head so much that I now can see the darkness of lightness" (6). A veteran echoes this same truth: "The world moves in a circle like a roulette wheel. In the beginning, black is on top, in the middle epochs, white holds the odds, but soon Ethiopia shall stretch forth her noble wings! Then place your money on the black!" (80).

It is the narrator's oratorical skills that bring him to the attention of the Brotherhood whose scientific historicism is cloaked in terms suggestive of an impending class war. When the narrator witnesses the eviction of an elderly couple, he is quick to summon his speechmaking ability in pointing out the hypocrisy of the white power structure. He invokes a sense of unity among the dispossessed masses, referring to them as "brothers" while urging them to stage a peaceful protest against their oppressor: "Yes, these old folks had a dream book, but the pages went blank and it failed to give them the number. It was called the Seeing Eye, The Great Constitutional Dream Book, The Secrets of Africa, The Wisdom of Egypt—but the eye was blind, it lost its luster. It's all cataracted like a cross-eyed carpenter and it doesn't saw straight. All we have is the Bible and this Law here rules that out. So where do we Go? Where do we go from here, without a pot—" (273). The narrator's fiery impromptu speech reminds the Harlemites of their exclusion and mobilizes them to action.

When the Harlem race riot erupts, ironically enough, on the fourth of July, the event foregrounds the failure of America's promises and becomes a war of words as much as one between people and ideologies. Seven, the biblical number suggestive of completion, has recurred throughout the narrator's journey, foreshadowing his rejection of an imposed reality: he receives seven letters of expulsion; there are seven tanks of liquid in the paint factory; the narrator sees seven mannequins hanging in front of a gutted storefront; and during the riot, he runs toward Seventh Avenue. Much to the narrator's surprise, Dupre, a man "outside the scheme till now," emerges spontaneously as a leader of the frustrated Harlemites (521). Along with Schofield, another previously unknown figure, he organizes the rioting crowd as they burn down a rundown apartment building owned and managed by whites. Ras the Destroyer declares "The time has come!" (474). Literally running for his life at this point, the narrator reads a sign that prompts his rejection of history: "'The time is Now . . . ,' the sign across the river began, but with history stomping upon me with hobnailed boots, I thought with a laugh, why worry about time?" (521).

The riot is ambiguously a celebration with blues and "shouts of laughter and disapproval" (532). A woman on top of a Borden milk wagon drinks beer and sings. In parody of the North-as-promised-land myth, oil, milk, and beer flow through the streets. Sirens roar and police on horseback arrive to end the disturbance. At the height of the conflict, the narrator hears an anonymous runner who recaptures the turbulent events of the evening: "Time's flying / Souls dying / The coming of the Lord / Draweth niiiigh!" (541).

While attempting to reason with Ras, the narrator discovers that he "had no words and no eloquence" (546). His throwing the spear which locks Ras's jaws suggests his refusal of Ras's fiery apocalyptic rhetoric. Once he is situated in his basement retreat, the narrator, a master storyteller, recounts the events of his past and concludes his tale with a chorus of affirmations. He insists that he is not a bitter man. Instead, in the process of the telling of his tale he has learned to love. During the course of his experiences he has gained an ironic distance from the painful events of his life.

The narrative is thus what Ellison refers to as "an autobiographical chronicle of personal catastrophe expressed lyrically" (Shadow and Act 78–79). Rejecting Ras's nationalism and Brother Jack's scientific historicism, the narrator relies instead upon the verbal skills emanating from his rural southern past. Thus, he recaptures the blueslike absurdity of modern America and the apocalypse toward which the nation is moving. Ellison's contribution to the African-American apocalypse is profoundly insistent, richly complex lyricism rooted in black oral expression—one which lends emphasis to the novel's ambiguous closing question: "Who knows but that, on the lower frequencies, I speak for you?" (568).

CHAPTER **4** James Baldwin, *Go Tell It on the Mountain*

> *It seemed to me that God himself had devised, to mark my father's end, the most sustained and brutally dissonant of codas. And it seemed to me, too, that the violence which rose all about us as my father left the world had been devised as a corrective for the pride of his eldest son. I had declined to believe in that apocalypse which had been central to my father's vision; very well, life seemed to be saying, here is something that will certainly pass for an apocalypse until the real thing comes along.*
>
> James Baldwin, *Notes of a Native Son*

As a novel of the great migration, James Baldwin's *Go Tell It on the Mountain* fictionalizes the historic move north and the disillusionment of those in search of freedom in an urban promised land. Baldwin's acute social consciousness prompts a rejection of the notion that fulfillment is to be found in the city. The Grimes family faces the same kinds of difficulties in the North that it confronts in the South. As a result, the text mirrors closely a black reality and subverts the apocalyptic vision present in Judeo-Christianity and the eschatological framework on which that vision is based.

Apocalypse and Ascent

Narrative action in James Baldwin's first novel *Go Tell It on the Mountain* is framed within the context of the storefront Pentecostal church, an arena that Baldwin, a former preacher and stepson of a minister, knew intimately. Gospel lyrics, portions of Scripture, even familial relationships in the novel point to the important role that the church has played in shaping the consciousness of black America. Despite his well-known quarrel with orthodox Christianity, Baldwin was never able to disengage himself from the church on an emotional level and much of his writing reveals the influence of this institution. It is his apocalyptic vision, an important though overlooked aspect of his work, that is arguably the most illuminating in an understanding of his art and politics.[1] Baldwin's conflict with the church as a social construct along with his disavowal of paternal influences, in both a literary and familial sense, led to the creation of an apocalypse that is decidedly secular and reflective of the group experiences of twentieth-century black America.

The many endings and beginnings in the text occur on both an individual and group level and are relevant to the struggle for selfhood, identity, and wholeness. Ironically, all paths lead to the church where the characters face the difficulties each tries to escape. Here, in what appears to be a shelter from the urban storm, the characters must work out, in a very real way, their soul salvation. Each must develop an appropriate means of coping with the contradictions of life in a society that promises freedom, opportunity, and progress, yet denies those privileges to the urban black masses. As much as any other space, it is the church that brings to remembrance the historic injustices blacks in white America have endured. It is where the saints gather to rehearse the rituals born out of the black struggle for survival in a hostile world. No matter how earnestly each of the characters tries, however, there is no deliverance from the ghetto and its dangers, and the church thus becomes both a safety valve and a snare.

The moment of faith, the point toward which the saints move, is the decisive event that is to mark a new beginning—the end of the old, unregenerative life and the start of a new life as a member of the household of faith. But the conversion experience comes with a great cost. It is accompanied by a realization of racial injustice and anger as a result of past wrongs. Baldwin's own conversion offers a gloss for reading those of the Grimes family. Motivated by a desire to best his tyrannical stepfather, find a refuge from the Harlem ghetto, and suppress his burgeoning sexuality, he fell sway to the powerful preaching of a woman evangelist.[2] Baldwin recounts his anguish when, later as a preacher, he tried to reconcile the otherworldly aspect of the Christian faith with the socioeconomic situation of the impoverished Harlemites: "Therefore, when I faced a congregation, it began to take all the strength I had not to stammer, not to curse, not to tell them to throw away their Bibles and get off their knees and go home and organize, for example, a rent strike. When I watched all the children, their copper, brown, and beige faces staring up at me as I taught Sunday School, I felt that I was committing a crime in talking about the gentle Jesus, in telling them to reconcile themselves to their misery on earth in order to gain the crown of eternal life" (*The Fire Next Time* 53).

In the fictional world that Baldwin creates, the moment of faith occasions a race consciousness insistent in its demand for a means of addressing racial wrongs, and it is the church that has the potential to serve as an arena for positive sociopolitical change. As congregation leader and divine spokesperson, the preacher is to lead the masses in the call for an end to racial injustice. The position is an exalted one influencing not only black but white society as well. The title that Baldwin chose for the novel is drawn from a popular Christmas carol announcing the birth of Christ and is richly suggestive of the preacher's authoritative position as one who, as God's mouthpiece safely positioned on the mountain, would dare to denounce racial wrongs. Such a position carries with it a great deal of responsibility, however. The preacher is to use his or her divine authority as a means of liberating the race.

Ascent, on a literal and symbolic level, and apocalypse are thus closely linked in the linguistic fabric of the text. The social elevation accompanying the divine call into the ministry is to bring about a much-needed reversal of the prevailing social order. Gabriel Grimes knows this prior to his conversion. Acutely aware of the restrictions that southern society places upon the African-American male, Gabriel wants to be free of the limitations whites impose and find the recognition he has been denied. Until the time he gets saved, Gabriel is given to the worldly lifestyle of those outside the protective arena of the church. Much of his time and energy is spent drinking, carousing, and womanizing. Baldwin would have the reader believe that the only real release from the monotonous routine of toiling for a white family and carousing comes when Gabriel must return home in the evenings and face his pious mother Rachel, whose deathbed wish is to see her only son saved. Gabriel prolongs his reckless lifestyle as long as he can until, at last, the pressures in and outside of the Grimes home force him to the altar of the Lord.

Given the dismal circumstances in which he lives, Gabriel has no choice but to get saved and join the church. If the collective experiences of the other male characters in the text are any indication of the degree of acceptance which black males find in the larger society, then Gabriel's dramatic moment of salvation may well have saved not only his soul but his life. Royal is recklessly defiant, unafraid of blacks or whites, and flaunts his disregard for authority. Gabriel's encounter with his estranged son highlights the young man's bold, brash, rebellious tendencies. When Gabriel learns that his son has been killed in a barroom brawl in Chicago, the revelation comes as no surprise. There are few other fates that could befall a black man who is so openly defiant of white rule. Richard, Elizabeth's headstrong lover, chooses to commit suicide rather than deal with the degradation associated with his arrest and beating at the hands of white police officers. His brilliance and persistent questioning of the established moral order of white society result in his early, tragic death and the unfulfilled potential associated with his deferred dreams of one day being more than a grocery clerk or an elevator boy.

The most graphic symbol suggestive of the fate awaiting the assertive black male is the murdered, castrated soldier that Gabriel sees in the rural South. Still in uniform, the soldier is a victim of the kind of life-threatening violence to which African-American men in the region were often subject. Society both hates and fears black masculinity. If he is to become one of the saints, John must suppress his nascent sexuality in order to find genuine acceptance among other believers. Father James, a figure for church authority, issues a stern "public warning" after learning that Elisha and Ella Mae have been dating.[3] The church leader fears that their relationship, however innocent at present, will lead to sexual sin. The message Baldwin conveys is that the church, like white society, has betrayed African-American men because of a call for self-denial in the pursuit of spirituality.

As a result of the church's historic betrayal of African Americans, Gabriel, whose name brings to mind the messenger angel who heralds the birth of Christ, learns that his desire for an authoritative voice is filled with contradictions: "Yes, he wanted power—he wanted to know himself to be the Lord's anointed, His well-beloved, and worthy, nearly, of that snow-white dove which had been sent down from Heaven to testify that Jesus was the Son of God. He wanted to be master, to speak with that authority which could only come from God" (94). The painful discovery Gabriel makes is that the leaders in the church are hypocrites. Following his emotionally charged sermon at the Twenty-Four Elders' Revival, an event which parodies Revelation's account of the twenty-four elders gathered around the throne, Deborah is proud to see Gabriel "mounted so high!" (107). Yet Gabriel feels out of place in the company of elders, many of whom are just as worldly as the sinners they condemn. Deborah becomes the object of their scorn because of her rape. The pompous elders see her as a fallen woman who is unworthy of black male attention.

The Twenty-Four Elders' Revival allows Gabriel a glimpse into his own future as a preacher. Baldwin expresses his disillusionment with the church when he writes that "the principles were Blindness, Loneliness, and Terror, the first principle necessarily and actively cultivated in order to deny the two others. I would love to believe that the principles were Faith, Hope, and Charity, but this is clearly not so for most Christians, or for what we call the Christian world" (*The Fire Next Time* 45). Gabriel has a dream in which a mysterious voice tells him to "Come up higher" (111), but that voice, like the one John hears while on the dusty temple floor, is misleading. Gabriel can have no real future in an institution whose beliefs are at odds with the needs of the masses.

The authoritative voice that Gabriel desires eludes him, and as Robert Bone suggests, "In exchange for the power of the Word, [Gabriel] trades away the personal power of his sex and the social power of his people" (220). Gabriel has a certain social mobility while he is in the rural South. But it is because he is a preacher and therefore not perceived as being a threat to the white power structure that he is able to move about unmolested. Whites feel that they can control Gabriel. When he realizes his impotence in the face of white rule, he becomes angry. Even so, he dare not openly challenge white society by speaking out against racial oppression. Gabriel only "dreamed of the feel of a white man's forehead against his shoe" (142).

Once he arrives in Harlem, Gabriel is in a fallen state. He lives out the fate that Esther pronounces in her letter when she prophesies that he will "be brought low one of these fine days" (135). Gabriel, although he is both a preacher and a father, has refused to openly acknowledge his illegitimate son Royal. Florence's urge to "rise up and tell it, tell everybody, about the blood the Lord's anointed is got on his hands" (214), would complete Gabriel's descent, but the novel closes with that plan of vengeance unresolved. Instead of accepting responsibility for his wrongs, Gabriel projects his failures onto those around him—Elizabeth and John.

John's motives in becoming saved are relevant to his desire to challenge Gabriel's rule in the church and the Grimes home. Indeed, in the novel's closing section the youth sees in Elisha's unknown tongue a possible weapon that he could use in confounding Gabriel. John's conversion, like that of his stepfather, then, is rooted in the need for paternal disavowal with religious, biological, and literary implications. Baldwin, for instance, was critical of the attempt on the part of the literary establishment to suggest Richard Wright as a literary father to black writers.[4] Something of his authorial rebellion figures into his treatment of the father-son relationship in *Go Tell It on the Mountain*. Early in the novel, in a scene reminiscent of the temptation of Christ, John stands atop a hill in Central Park exulting in the power and opportunities the city proffers. At the same time he realizes that he can never enjoy life in white New York. In spite of his intellect and ambition, he is what Baldwin refers to as "a bastard of the West" (Notes of a Native Son 4).

Each member of the Grimes family strives for inclusion in the social mainstream, only to be confronted with racial realities: Elizabeth's fair-skinned mother shuns her; Florence uses bleaching creme in order to lighten her beautiful dark skin; and Gabriel refers to John as being black, ugly, and Satanic. For them, religion is, as Robert Bone puts it, "a kind of spiritual bleaching creme" (223).

John's conversion in Part Three occurs in terms relevant to his realization of the historic role that Christianity has played in perpetuating black exclusion. The mysterious voices and visions which he witnesses are suggestive of what Geneva Smitherman refers to as the push-pull tension between black culture, or the church, and American culture, represented by the city (63). A malicious, ironic voice insists that John "rise—and, at once, to leave this temple and go out into the world" (193). In the midst of his ordeal, he becomes aware of the legacy which white Christianity bequeaths to the black male: "He did not know where he was. There was silence everywhere—only a perpetual, distant, faint trembling far beneath him—the roaring, perhaps, of the fires of Hell, over which he was suspended, or the echo, persistent, invincible still, of the moving feet of the saints. He thought of the mountaintop, where he longed to be, where the sun would cover him like a cloth of gold, would cover his head like a crown of fire, and in his hands he would hold a living rod. But this was no mountain where John lay, here, no robe, no crown. And the living rod was uplifted in other hands" (196).

It is at the height of his conversion that John hears the voice of Elisha whose unknown tongue is the language of love and unconditional acceptance that will confound Gabriel. Shortly thereafter, like John the Revelator in exile on Patmos, he sees the city: "I, John, saw a city, way in the middle of the air, / Waiting, waiting, waiting up there" (204). Sadly, though, John is unable to speak "the authoritative, the living word" that would bridge the gap between himself and his stepfather (207). His long-awaited testimony is a repetition of his Gabriel's text: "My witness is in Heaven and my record is on high" (207).

As the text closes, a central question that remains involves the nature of John's role in the church. Although the saints are jubilant at John's conversion, Baldwin's starkly realistic description of the Harlem ghetto suggests that the youth will face the same kinds of problems after his salvation that he did prior to the event. John's eagerly anticipated rebirth will allow him only a temporary escape from the perils of ghetto life. His ascent to the mountain will be followed by a descent. Thus, the saints' jubilant admonition that John should "rise up and talk about the Lord's deliverance" (205) is tempered by Baldwin's own conversion experience, after which he concludes, "I found no answer on the floor" (*The Fire Next Time* 45).

Voices from the Pentecostal Church

If the moment of faith results in an ambivalence concerning a response to racial oppression, then the voices which issue forth from the church are equally as complex in their expression of black anger. Baldwin's use of Scripture as an intertext sheds light on the African-American journey from bondage to freedom.[5] The collective voices of Baldwin's troubled saints are united in their call for an end to the social, economic, and political injustices of life in an urban promised land. Narrative action thus begins on the Seventh Day, symbolically both the last day of Creation and the end of time and history. The epigraph for this section of the text is drawn from Revelation: "And the Spirit and the bride say, Come. / And let him that heareth say, Come. / And let him that is athirst come. / And whosoever will, let him take / the water of life freely." That Baldwin employs John's limited omniscient point of view as a narrative strategy in Parts One and Three allows the reader a unique perspective on the city. The world that the Grimes family inhabits is far-removed from the paradisal New Jerusalem which John the Revelator foresaw. Here, in Harlem, "the wages of sin were visible everywhere, in every wine-stained and urine-splashed hallway, in every clanging ambulance bell, in every scar on the faces of the pimps and their whores, in every helpless, newborn baby being brought into this danger, in every knife and pistol fight on the Avenue, and in every disastrous bulletin" (*The Fire Next Time* 34).

Baldwin's juxtaposition of Scripture with the largely oral modes of expression which undergird the novel results in creative revisioning of biblical texts. That juxtaposition not only underscores the failure of the church to address the needs of the urban masses but points to the social function of religion among African Americans as what Baldwin calls "a complete and exquisite fantasy revenge" (*Notes of a Native Son* 54). It is Florence's prayer that foregrounds the trek north. Her lifelong ambition is to escape the place that southern patriarchy prescribes for women. Gabriel is well-fed, well-clothed, and well-educated, while Florence must remain at home attending to domestic duties. An ex-slave who has spent her time cooking and cleaning for whites, Rachel Grimes accepts her place in a rigidly stratified southern hierarchy and encourages her daughter to follow in her footsteps. Women, as far as Rachel is concerned, are to subordinate their needs and aspirations to those of men. Florence's best friend Deborah has no identity apart from that the church assigns. After her rape, she is a community outcast, caring for the needs of Rachel and Gabriel.

Florence's decision to journey north results from her desire to move beyond the life of childbearing and endless toil to which women in the South were subject. Yet she finds herself in a situation similar to the one she tries to avoid. While in the North she meets and marries Frank, a free-spirited man who reminds her of the vulnerabilities of womanhood. Frank is content with a life of gambling and drinking, eschewing the social uplift that is so important to Florence's middle-class aspirations. Her efforts at changing Frank so that he too is upwardly mobile are futile. At the end of their stormy ten-year marriage Frank is no closer to being the man Florence has wanted him to be than he was when they met.

When Frank dies, Florence faces the fate she tried to avoid. She and Elizabeth are forced to work among the "common niggers" Florence dislikes (67). Florence, who is dying of cancer, is not only without the light, life, and healing that the song lyrics introducing her prayer encode, she has forgotten how to pray. She remembers that her mother's formula for effective prayer includes emptying one's heart of malice toward one's enemies, but Florence is either unable or unwilling to forgive Gabriel for the pain he has caused her. Her fear is that she will die before gaining vengeance on her brother.

The individual narratives in Part Two, thinly disguised as prayers, offer the reader insight into the psychologies of the members of the Grimes family, each of whom is betrayed by a naive belief in the possibility of attaining a futuristic reward. Even the characters' favorite Scriptures are ironic. Gabriel's is "set thine house in order," yet his house is anything but orderly. Elizabeth's is "and we know that all things work together for good to them who love the Lord," but the trials of life appear to work against her.

More than any other aspect of novel, however, it is the sermonic discourse from the Pentecostal Church that issues the strongest indictment of white society and the clearest statement of the black awareness of social injustice. During the Twenty-Four Elders' Revival, Gabriel's sermon, based on the sixth chapter of Isaiah, has to do with unclean lips. This same text serves as an epigraph for Part Three: "Then said I, Woe is me! for I am undone; / because I am a man of unclean lips, / and I dwell in the midst of a people / of unclean lips; for mine eyes have / seen the King, the Lord of hosts." Only after his tragic fall following his affair with Esther is Gabriel able to make an association between sin and the collective plight of blacks in the West. Gabriel's fall occurs in terms relevant to his acceptance of the collective dispossession of the race. For the first time in his life, he experiences a oneness between himself and other African Americans searching in vain for acceptance in Western society. The only real hope that Baldwin's saints have is for a reversal of their plight. Thus, the epigraph for Part Two, "The Prayers of the Saints," is drawn from the Book of Revelation and expresses the desire on the part of the martyred remnant for vengeance: "And they cried with a loud voice, saying, / How long, O Lord, holy and true, / dost thou not judge and avenge our blood / on them that dwell on the earth?"

On the morning of the eighth day the saints return home following the evening tarry service. Despite their jubilant mood, Baldwin's focus on the harsh realities of life in the Harlem ghetto underscores the irony of their belief in new life after the moment of faith. John will face the same problems after his conversion that he faced before. The saints hear "an ambulance siren, and a crying bell" (218), evidence of imminent secular doom. The morning sun begins to "corrupt with fire" (213). Only John and Elisha are to escape the coming apocalypse, however. Having formed a bond based on mutual acceptance and unconditional love, they, alone, are of the elect. As the narrative closes, then, "The sun . . . fell over Elisha like a golden robe and struck John's forehead, where Elisha had kissed him, like a seal ineffaceable forever" (221).

The Fire This Time: Ritual Cleansings and Purifications

Consistent with a black theological position, Baldwin's writings reveal a refusal of compensatory Christianity. Eschatology, a controversial aspect of orthodox religion, is therefore reversed in Go Tell It on the Mountain. What concerns Baldwin is not so much the events which, according to Revelation, are to occur in the future. Rather, the text reveals the suffering which the Grimes family endures in the present. Water and fire, biblical symbols associated with apocalypse, are interwoven throughout the text and suggest the difficulties the saints encounter while journeying toward their promised land. Their entrance into this mythical place has much to do with their acceptance of tests and trials along the way.

The name that Baldwin chooses for the family's place of worship, the Temple of the Fire Baptized, is especially fitting. Each member endures horrendous suffering before being counted worthy to worship at the altar of the Lord. John is only faintly aware of the fate awaiting him once he joins the company of believers. He, too, will be among those whom society considers an outcast. That Gabriel refers to John as being black, ugly, and Satanic speaks of the extent to which John's stepfather has internalized Western ideals. The Grimes family can never be acceptable on the terms that white society establishes. In a scene involving John's frustrating attempt to rid his home of its invincible filth, the novel evokes the Grimes family's inner torment. Baldwin recaptures the psychic tension resulting from the sense of twoness which, according to W. E. B. Du Bois, characterizes black life in white America (45). In spite of their efforts at socioeconomic progress, the Grimes family fails to move forward toward inclusion in the social mainstream. They remain in a helllike existence with no possibility for release.

Florence taunts Gabriel about his destiny in the next life, but the suffering that he endures in the present is just as intense as that awaiting sinners in the hereafter. Robert Bone is correct in his assertion that "the substance of Gabriel's life is moral evasion" (224). Gabriel lives in a state of guilt and isolation, mainly because of his failure to acknowledge openly his son Royal. Not once does he accept responsibility for his affair with Esther. Their coupling occurs in a context with the two "burning beside the sink" and is suggestive of the atmosphere of hell (126). As a result of Gabriel's moral failure, Esther has to raise her son alone. When she dies, Royal returns to the South where he grows up as a stranger to his father and God. His rebellion, much like that of the youthful Gabriel, is a mockery of the Christian ideals of the church.

No matter how hard Baldwin's saints try, they cannot escape the sins of the flesh, and much of the torment that the characters experience occurs because of their failed attempts to suppress their carnal nature. On the morning of his conversion, Gabriel is leaving a harlot's house; Florence is unable to resists Frank's appeal to her femininity; and Elizabeth, once outside of her aunt's restrictive home, indulges her passions with Richard. Florence best sums up the tension between the flesh and the spirit: "But I don't care how many times you change your ways," Florence tells Gabriel, "what's in you is in you, and it's got to come out" (180).

Thus, in light of the day-to-day trials that the characters endure, the rainstorm which occurs during the evening tarry service is no less fierce than the personal crises the saints face. Gabriel copes with his guilt by projecting it onto Elizabeth and John. It is Florence, however, who insists that Gabriel assume responsibility for his sins. She places the blame for his actions squarely on his own shoulders: "You still promising the Lord you going to do better—and you think whatever you done already, whatever you doing right at that minute, don't count. Of all the men I ever knew, you's the man who ought to be hoping the Bible's all a lie—'cause if that trumpet ever sounds, you going to spend eternity talking" (214–15).

Much of the emotional trauma taking place within the narrative happens in the lives of Baldwin's female characters whose collective plight suggests they suffer the double oppression of racism and sexism. Each of them, as Trudier Harris points out, is extremely vulnerable within a patriarchal system (Black Women in the Fiction of James Baldwin 12). Whether it is the stoic Deborah, stigmatized because of rape, or Esther, who is labeled a loose woman because of her failure to live up to society's puritanical standards, the women who people Baldwin's text are at a marked disadvantage. They are forced to bear the brunt of the sins of the race. "The menfolk, they die, and its all over for them," Florence tells Elizabeth, "but we women, we have to keep on living and try to forget what they done to us" (182).

Rachel Grimes perpetuates the values of a patriarchal society by giving Gabriel preferential treatment. "There was only one future in that house," the omniscient narrator tells the reader in Florence's "prayer," "and it was Gabriel's—to which, since Gabriel was a manchild, all else must be sacrificed" (72). Florence is forced to sacrifice her goals for Gabriel's burgeoning masculinity. Her early years are spent caring for her ailing mother while Gabriel is out sowing his wild oats. When Florence is no longer present, Deborah becomes Rachel's nursemaid, again freeing Gabriel to pursue his worldly lifestyle. Society's expectations for women in the rural South therefore consign the women to subservient positions in the home and church. Deborah remains the passive, devoted pastor's wife, despite her knowledge of her husband's infidelity. Her only means of venting her pain upon learning of Gabriel's betrayal is by writing a letter to her best friend Florence.

Among the members of the older generation of the Grimes family, it is Elizabeth who has best come to terms with the harsh realities of life, and as she watches John at the tarry service, her heart is filled with an awareness of the tests and trials that await him. During his initiation ordeal, which occurs amidst fire, flood, and darkness, he witnesses a number of visions foretelling his fate. Only as he accepts the fiery tests in the future is his salvation brought to a closure. John sees a great company of believers. They are the dispossessed black masses: "They were the despised and rejected, the wretched and the spat upon, the earth's offscouring; and he was in their company, and they would swallow up his soul. The stripes they had endured would scar his back, their punishment would be his, their portion his, his their humiliation, anguish, chains, their dungeon his, their death his. . . . And their dread testimony would be his!" (201). When John obeys the saints' veiled urging to "go through this fire" he is saved (202). By identifying with them in their suffering, he finds new life. As if to indicate John's transformation, the novel closes with a focus on the liberating bond established between John and Elisha, a type of Christ the Redeemer whose presence is to usher in a new era of harmony and love.

Given the autobiographical dimensions of narrative action, there is no reason to believe that John's ethereal salvation experience will last. Baldwin remained in the church only three years before deciding to pursue his goals of becoming a writer. John makes what is a temporary peace with the social forces at work against him in the Harlem ghetto. Even so, *Go Tell It on the Mountain* is a powerful testament to the redeeming value of love and unconditional acceptance, a theme to which Baldwin would return in his later works. Only through practicing the kind of acceptance which John and Elisha exhibit can there be any hope for arresting the cycle of history leading to what Baldwin refers to as a "cosmic vengeance" soon to be visited upon America (*The Fire Next Time* 119). Baldwin, a stern yet sensitive social commentator, hopes to raise the consciousness of his black and white audiences in order to forestall the fire next time.

CHAPTER 5

LeRoi Jones [Imamu Amiri Baraka],
The System of Dante's Hell

> *The Black Artist's role in America is to aid in the destruction of America as he*
> *knows it. His role is to report and reflect so precisely the nature of the society, and*
> *of himself in that society, that other men will be moved by the exactness of his*
> *rendering and, if they are black men, grow strong through this moving, having*
> *seen their own strength, and weakness; and if they are white men, tremble, curse,*
> *and go mad, because they will be drenched with the filth of their evil.*
>
> LeRoi Jones, *Home: Social Essays*

As a leading spokesperson among Black Arts writers, LeRoi Jones (Imamu
Amiri Baraka) is concerned with the destruction of a scriptocentric art form
that has roots in Western society and the creation of an art that reflects an
African-American reality. *The System of Dante's Hell* is an experimental work of
fiction in which Jones draws upon aspects of black expressive culture in
the creation of a world order privileging the black experience.

The Last Days of the American Empire

When Addison Gayle Jr. called for a literature that would reflect the group
aspirations of African Americans, he expressed the artistic credo that serves
as a guiding impulse in the fiction, nonfiction prose, poetry, and drama of
LeRoi Jones (*The Black Aesthetic* 393). At once a prophet, social critic, revolutionary, and talented creative artist, Jones combines his varied personae in
the writing of *The System of Dante's Hell*, an intriguing work of fiction whose
critical reception shows the problems posed when black artists attempt to
distill the material of a culture that is largely oral into written form.[1] The
novel is based loosely on Dante's *Inferno*, but a search for a deeper meaning
leads the reader away from a consideration of Dante's schematization of
hell as a posthumous reality and the entire Judeo-Christian eschatological

system out of which that scheme evolves. Notions of morality central to Medieval society offer a gloss for reading the constant, unrelieved, and more immediate chaos of contemporary America. Jones's concern is with the myriad ways in which the American system, with its tendency toward categorization based on race, class, and gender, fosters among African Americans a psychological turmoil that is just as debilitating as an otherworldly hell.

The novel's autobiographical dimensions are obvious enough, but what critics fail to acknowledge is that Jones is not merely chronicling his own personal experiences. Rather, his is an account of a spiritual journey, with epic overtones, toward the development of a black consciousness. The epilogue "Sound and Image" stresses the psychosocial implications of narrative action: "Hell in the head. The torture of being the unseen object, and, the constantly observed subject. The flame of social dichotomy. Split open down the center, which is the early legacy of the black man unfocused on blackness. The dichotomy of what is seen and taught and desired opposed to what is felt."[2]

Jones translates into art what Abdul JanMohammed describes as the Manichaean tensions between black and white, self and other, present in a colonized setting (1–12). In the fictional world of the novel, the legacy that white society bequeaths African Americans is a deep-seated self-hatred stemming from the notion that all that is good, acceptable, or desirable is a product of the West. Because of the feelings of unworthiness blacks might feel by virtue of their internalization of white values, they may be inclined to deny aspects of black culture in the pursuit of the white ideal. Such a situation leads ultimately to frustration, however, for to accept a culture produced by whites as the only valid culture is to reject one's true self.

Jones tests the reality of his thesis by placing Roi, his fictional self, into a series of situations which prompt him to choose either his ethnic past or aspects of American culture. On several occasions Roi fails to recognize the value of the past that has molded his character until he is at last forced to accept his blackness. The text could be divided into two distinct segments, each one representing a phase in the hero's psychological development: the preconscious and the conscious phase. At first Roi is emotionally detached from his ghetto home, a wasteland with its poverty, decadence, and filth. Those who live in the ghetto are imprisoned and have little or no opportunity for upward socioeconomic mobility. For those fortunate enough to be able to escape the ghetto and gain entry into the social mainstream, there remains still another, more subtle, form of imprisonment—that occasioned by life in racially polarized America. Jones's thematic focus on the identity crisis faced by the emerging black middle class prompts his improvisation upon Dante: whereas Dante's hell exists on a vertical plane in the next life, as Jones envisions it, hell is thisworldly and is a horizontal reality. For blacks in white America, all of life, all of existence, is hell.[3]

The particular evil that Roi is guilty of early in the text is his failure to embrace the vitality of ghetto life. Here, the reader is able to discern something of Jones's rather ambivalent portrayal of the ghetto. Even though the urban arena is a limiting environment that contributes to black aimlessness and despair, at the same time it embodies a certain life noticeably absent in Western culture. Blues, the dozens, and signifying are verbal arts central to Roi's youth, and Jones relies heavily upon these forms of expression in crafting the text. The ghetto spawns the culture that Roi must acknowledge if he is to be whole.

Thus, in "Neutrals: the Vestibule," Roi remains distanced, in psychological terms, from the urban arena and all that it signifies. He is among the uninitiated—the neutrals—who are in, but not really a part of, ghetto life. His dispassionate description of his environment shows just how far removed he is from the black world:

> The neutrals run jewelry shops & shit in silence under magazines. Women disappear into Canada. They painted & led interminable lives. They marched along the sides of our cars in the cold brown weather. They wore corduroy caps & listened to portables. The world was in their eyes. They wore rings & had stories about them. They walked halfway back from school with me. They were as tall as anyone else you knew. Some sulked, across the street out of sight, near the alley where the entrance to his home was. A fat mother. A fat father with a mustache. Both houses, and the irishman's near the playground. Balls went in our yards. Strong hitters went in Angel's. They all lived near everything. (9–10)

Jones satirizes all of society in evoking what is America's last days, a time of social anarchy and moral failure. His indictment of contemporary America is double-edged: on the one hand, he is critical of blacks who have sacrificed their identities in the pursuit of middle-class success; on the other, he holds white society up for scrutiny because of its perpetuation of the social, economic, and political conditions which prompt African Americans to seek fulfillment apart from their ethnic past.

Although narrative focus is on the lives of African Americans, white society exerts its powerful influence. Roi shows the extent to which he has internalized white standards by his preference for light-skinned women and the list of authors whose works he reads. The hero's literary tastes are dictated by the white establishment: "The first guy he spoke to me grinning and I said my name was Stephen Dedalus. And I read Proust and mathematics and loved Eliot for his tears. Towers, like Yeats (I didn't know him then, or only a little because of the Second Coming & Leda)" (58).

Elsewhere, Jones speaks frankly about the betrayal of the American educational system. "Having read all of whitie's books, I wanted to be an authority on them," he mentions. "Having been taught that art was 'what white men did,' I almost became one, to have a go at it. Having been the only 'middle-class' chump running with the Hillside Place bads, I was 'saved' from them by my parents' determination and the cool scholarship game which turns stone killers pure alabaster by graduation time. Having been born October 7, my nature was to listen to everybody, to be sensitive to, and look at, everything" (*Home* 10).

Only after Roi acquires the psychological maturity necessary to revise his earlier attitude toward himself and his place in society does he acknowledge the extent to which he has internalized white culture. His awakening leads to self-loathing: "I am myself. Insert the word disgust. A verb. Get rid of the 'am.' Break out. Kill it. Rip the thing to shreds. This thing, if you read it, will jam your face in my shit. Now say something intelligent!" (15).

Instead of alleviating the social chaos pervasive in contemporary America, the institutions of society—the family and church—further the dislocation taking place. Roi goes through the rites of manhood largely within the context of his boyhood gang, "The Secret Seven," whose name is revealing of Jones's apocalyptic intentions in writing. The members of the gang engage in activities that are both destructive and self-destructive. Parental supervision during Roi's coming of age is virtually nonexistent, and he defines himself almost exclusively in relation to other boys in the ghetto.

Like James Baldwin, Jones is critical of orthodox Christianity because of its failure to meet the socioeconomic needs of the urban masses. As if to indicate the text's pervasive anti-Christian emphasis, he places the Christians in the section entitled "The Ninth Ditch: the Makers of Discord." "Hypocrite(s)" deals more directly with the role of the church in the black experience. The narrator is conscious of hierarchical distinctions, evidenced by where one is allowed to sit during worship services: "Their grandsons would watch from the balcony (if you were middleclass baptists & had some women with pince-nez)" (61). Those who are among the working class are held in low esteem: "Rufus the bootblack, low man on the totem pole" (62). The worshipers internalize the values and standards present in the larger society: "And Rudy's mother was ugly and looked up to my grandmother, so that made him lower. Place. Place each thing, each dot of life. Each person, will be PLACED. DISPOSED OF" (63–64).

The church offers a much-needed emotional release for ghetto dwellers whose daily existence is a constant reminder of black powerlessness. Shouting or stealing are the only available avenues of expression for the displaced masses. The larger society has placed them in a social context which limits opportunities for achievement. In addition, there is materialism among those in positions of power and authority: "The trustees filed in smiling. After they'd brought in the huge baskets of money. They'd smile & be important" (61). Appropriately, as if to indicate the pretensions among worshipers, the section closes with a short drama.

The narrative is structured around the varied forms of evil Roi's search for social acceptance assumes. In "Treachery to Kindred" there is an account of an attempted gang rape. Roi, who is a college student at the time, has bought into the American myth of success: "THE BEAUTIFUL MIDDLE-CLASS HAD FORMED AND I WAS TO BE A GREAT FIGURE, A GIANT AMONG THEM" (107). The woman in the section, "an actual damned soul" (116), embodies the decadence of the ghetto environment, and Roi's callous disregard for her suffering is an indicator of the indifference on the part of the middle class. Roi is at first passive but still morally responsible in the aborted gang rape: "They made to laugh. They made to get into the car. They made not be be responsible. All with me. (Tho this is new, I tell you now because, somehow, it all is right, whatever. For what sin you find me here. It's mine. My own irreconcilable life. My blood. My footsteps towards the black car smeared softly in the slow shadows of leaves.) The houses shone like naked bulbs. Thin laughter from the party trailed us up the street" (111). By the end of the section, however, he is an active and willing participant. His friends rally around him—a future middle-class leader—as the woman escapes them.

With his deconstructionist rewriting of Dante's Inferno, Jones directs the reader's focus of attention to the social chaos that is contemporary America's distinctive feature. Jones's art is therefore intensely political, and the novel form becomes the medium through which the creative artist is to usher in a new black consciousness that has its basis in the music and language of African Americans.[4] Jones's comments regarding his dramatic works points to the apocalyptic ethic at the heart of his writing. "This is a theatre of assault," he writes regarding the revolutionary theater. "The play that will split the heavens for us will be called THE DESTRUCTION OF AMERICA. The heroes will be Crazy Horse, Denmark Vesey, Patrice Lumumba, and not history, not memory, not sad sentimental groping for a warmth in our despair; these will be men, new heroes, and their enemies most of you who are reading this" (*Home* 215). Roi's journey through contemporary America, then, is one in which the artist-narrator's evolving black consciousness heralds a possible end to the hegemony predominantly white literary establishment creates; the American empire is the authority white society assumes.[1]

Jones extends his critique of white society to include an indictment of its ruthless annihilation of Native Americans. The section entitled "Seven (The Destruction of America)," which is a careful admixture of poetry and prose, is anti-imperialist in its denouncement of genocide. All people of color are united through their victimization by white racism and the only viable solution to the race war is a violent overthrow of the social order.[5]

Ambivalent Flight

Jones welcomes the prospect of an apocalyptic reversal that would overthrow the prevailing social order. Such a reversal is to come about not through the presence of a divine agent, but as a result of the efforts of the socially conscious creative artist who is willing to embrace blackness as a means of redefining the self and society. Thus, the hero Roi's efforts at escaping the squalor and waste of the ghetto are at best futile. What he discovers is that he merely exchanges the ambivalent hell of ghetto life for the unequivocal hell of contemporary America. Jones, like most African-American novelists, turns topsy-turvy notions present in the American mythos that fulfillment is to be found by moving toward an American Eden. Only by delving into a culture that is indigenously black does Roi find wholeness. In the fictional world that Jones constructs, flight is relevant to the physical and spiritual journey the hero undertakes as he moves through the various systems and institutions of contemporary America. Like Daedalus, the legendary inventor of wings with whom Roi identifies, Roi has heroic aspirations. That he chooses to be an army pilot is a reflection of his desire to be a part of a fast-paced technological world. Once he is in the army, however, he must subordinate his individual aspirations to those of the group. In his attempt to achieve social status in the white world, Roi sacrifices his sense of self.

With its insistence on conformity and regimentation, the army functions as an extension of the same system that holds Roi in check. Hence, in the section which offers an account of the hero's army experience, "The Eighth Ditch (Is Drama," Roi and his comrades are assigned a number; each one is rendered invisible and anonymous. The section consists of dialogue between the hero and "64." As if to indicate the stasis that characterizes Roi's failed flight away from the past, the section opens and closes with the same scene: a dark army tent where the soldiers sleep. Their meandering conversation is punctuated with revealing truths. "64," who urges the reader to call him Herman, mentions the futility of "46's" moral evasion: "So buy expensive clothes and become middleclass that summer after college. But don't sneak away! You can't. I'll never know you, as some adventurer, but only as chattel. Sheep. A 'turkey,' in our vernacular" (80). The blueslike cadence of "64's" monologues place him at odds with the bookish "46," whose declaration that he can play the dozens does little to convince "64" or the reader of his black consciousness.

Moreover, the hero's sexual preference calls into question the role that he would assume as a member of the social mainstream. His flight away from the imprisonment of the ghetto has resulted in a symbolic emasculation represented by his homosexuality. "The black man in America has always been expected to function as less than a man," Jones comments regarding black masculinity. "This was taken for granted, and was the ugliest weight of his enslavement" (Home 221). The orgy with which the section ends indicates white society's strategy of pitting black men against each other in vying for meager sociopolitical rewards. Much like the blindfolded youths in the battle royal episode in Ralph Ellison's Invisible Man, the men are subjugated, stripped of all vestiges of social identity, and then forced to compete among themselves rather than against their real enemy, the white power structure.

Structurally, the narrative reflects the ambivalence associated with Roi's flight away from his ethnic past. Once he journeys south to the Bottom, a black community just outside of Shreveport, Louisiana, the hero's flight or moral evasion becomes more pronounced. Jones stresses his thematic focus on the search for identity by placing Roi in the deepest part of hell: "*I put The Heretics in the deepest part of hell, though Dante had them spared, on higher ground. It is heresy, against one's own sources, running in terror, from one's deepest responses and insights . . . the denial of feeling . . . that I see as basest evil."

Although the Bottom is the site of Roi's transformation, he is initially an outsider who is far removed from the community and its residents. His narrowly logical description of the sights, the sounds, and the people who reside there indicates the extent to which he has distanced himself from the black past:

> The place was filled with shades. Ghosts. And the huge ugly hands of actual spooks. Standing around the bar, spilling wine on greasy shirts. Yelling at a fat yellow spliv who talked about all their mothers, pulling out their drinks. Laughing with wet cigarettes and the paper stuck to fat lips. Crazy as anything in the world, and sad because of it. Yelling as not to hear the sad breathing world. Turning all music up. Screaming all lyrics. Tough black men . . . weak black men. Filthy drunk women whose perfume was cheap unnatural flowers. Quiet thin ladies whose lives had ended and whose teeth hung stupidly in their silent mouths . . . rotted by thousands of nickel wines. A smell of despair and drunkenness. Silence and laughter, and the sounds of their movement under it. Their frightening lives. (128)

The surreal atmosphere of this section of the text, which consists of "fast narrative," is compounded by Roi's confusion of identity. He is in a state of denial. Here, as he dances with Peaches in "the Joint," he comes close to realizing what Kimberly Benston sees as the dynamic energy that is characteristic of black culture (20–23):

> We danced, this face and I, close so I had her sweat in my mouth, her flesh the only sound my brain could use. Stinking, and the music over us like a sky, choked any other movement off. I danced. And my history was there, had passed no further. Where it ended, here, the light white talking jig, died in the arms of some sentry of Africa. Some short-haired witch out of my mother's most hideous dreams. I was nobody now, mama. Nobody. Any other secret nigger. No one the white world wanted or would look at. (129–30)

The confusion that Roi experiences is a necessary prelude to his spiritual rebirth. It is as if he must shed his old self before new life can begin. Peaches is then both guide and foreteller in the symbolic rebirth Roi undergoes and his new life parallels his unconditional acceptance of all that she embodies. Even though Roi finds her to be repulsive, she represents the essence of black folk culture. As the two interact, however, Roi identifies with white heroes: "Please you don't know me. Not what's in my head. I'm beautiful. Stephen Dedalus. A mind, here where there is only steel. Nothing else. Young pharaoh under trees. Young pharaoh, romantic, liar. Feel my face, how tender. My eyes. My soul is white, pure white, and soars. Is the God himself. This world and all others" (140).

With Peaches' assistance, Roi begins the journey toward self-acceptance. What he experiences in her dark, secluded basement is a ritualistic return to the womb not unlike that experienced by neophytes in non-Western cultures.[6] Roi descends, literally and symbolically, into the hell of black life. Having abandoned his former self, he is preparing for spiritual flight. Significantly, their affair is consummated with a sexual union that tests Roi's burgeoning manhood. He, at last, is ready to reenter the real world: "And I felt the world grow together as I hadn't known it. All lies before, I thought. All fraud and sickness. This was the world. It leaned under its own suns, and people moved on it. A real world. Of flesh, of smells, of soft black harmonies and color. The dead maelstrom of my head, a sickness (148).

Roi speaks of his rebirth in terms that are richly suggestive not just of a new self but a new world order as well—one that reflects a black reality. By journeying to the Bottom, Roi has moved outside of Western time and entered a new cosmology. Roi, now armed with a black consciousness, can then ascend, leaving the Bottom, but not its rich culture, behind. "I walked away from the house," he tells the reader. "Up the road, to go out of Bottom" (150).

The Search For Closure

In *The System of Dante's Hell*, as with much of African-American fictional discourse, the Bottom is more than just a geographical place; it functions metaphorically as a distinctly black reality, a self-contained system that is separate from the West. The novel's unresolved closure suggests the difficulties that Roi, the archetypal African American, faces when he tries to reconcile his ethnic past with the American present. While Jones acknowledges the value of the black cultural heritage, he also realizes the necessity of assuming what Ralph Ellison's nameless narrator calls a "socially responsible role." The central task confronting Roi as he leaves the Bottom is how to integrate his black consciousness into his existence as an American.

His task is not an easy one by any means. The narrative perspective Jones employs is one which emphasizes the recursive nature of time and history. Time, as it is represented, is synchronic rather than diachronic. "You can never be sure of the hour," the narrator reminds the reader in "The Diviners" (51). Real progress in the context of narrative action is to be measured in terms of the psychological growth Roi experiences instead of by his movement along a linear path. From the vantage point of age and maturity the narrator speaks of the events that lead to his present state: "You've done everything you said you wdn't. Everything you said you dispised. A fat mind, lying to itself'" (13). All of life is part of the same continuum, according to Jones. "I am and was and will be a social animal," Jones comments in "Sound and Image." The past is a part of the present.

If there is one symbol that indicates Jones's artistic concern with narrative endings it is his recurring use of seven which, as far as apocalypse is concerned, relates to the end of time and history. Roi is a member of a gang, "the Secret Seven," and the seventh person never arrives. Somehow the end is always deferred. Later, he tells the reader, "I control the Secret Seven" (81). In structural and thematic terms, his story begins and ends at roughly the same point: with his entry into the adult world. Key scenes recur, creating a narrative that is circular, not strictly linear. The sights and sounds present in the Bottom, for instance, remind Roi of his Newark ghetto home. In the Bottom as well as in Newark, Roi is a detached observer of and a participant in the hell of contemporary America. What emerges in the closing section is a new black consciousness on Roi's part as he decides to reenter white society.

Peaches can offer Roi a sense of culture and history, but it is also necessary for Roi to function socially. Roi must therefore incorporate the timeless mother wit and survival lessons Peaches imparts into a more integrated self. The "sweet grace" the hero finds is his ability to operate on two levels, not just one. Returning to white society has its perils, as Roi discovers when he is beaten by three black boys who call him "Mr. Half-white muthafucka" (151). That he wakes up two days later with white men screaming for God to help him is not to be interpreted as his abandonment of his new black consciousness. God, according to Jones, "is simply a white man, a white idea." Roi, who calls on God out of desperation, not faith, will never be the same as he was before his initiation ordeal.

The novel's ambiguous, unresolved closure conveys, then, to borrow Frank Kermode's phrase, "the sense of an ending." Roi descends into the depths of black life only to emerge later on a higher spiritual plane. The experience is not unlike a religious conversion similar to the one Jones himself underwent on the way to becoming Imamu Amiri Baraka. *The System of Dante's Hell* is therefore a written testament to the reality of that transformation, one that countless other African Americans in contemporary literature and life would undergo.

CHAPTER **6** Toni Morrison, Sula

> *As children of captivity we look forward to a new day and a new, yet ever old, land of our fathers, the land of refuge, the land of the Prophets, the land of the Saints, and the land of God's crowning glory. We shall gather together our children, our treasures and our loved ones, and, as the children of Israel, by the command of God, faced the promised land, so in time we shall also stretch forth our hands and bless our country.*
>
> Marcus Garvey, Speech delivered at Madison Square Garden, March 1924

Toni Morrison's *Sula* is structured around catastrophes of various sorts, from individual deaths to the destruction of the Bottom, which is razed in order to make room for a golf course. With each of them there is a projected return to a mythic past—much like Marcus Garvey's idealized Africa—where there is community, harmony, and freedom. Drawing upon an African cosmological system, Morrison maintains that although life in modern America is chaotic, it is possible to escape life in the West and recover the time of the black community's non-Western beginnings.

Modern Chaos and Ancient Paradigms

The destruction of the Bottom, a black community located in the hills above the fictional town of Medallion, Ohio, is a central event in Toni Morrison's *Sula*. With the collapse of a tunnel linking Medallion to a neighboring town and the leveling of the Bottom in order to make room for a golf course, the community appears to have reached its inevitable end. Those in the Bottom are attuned to natural phenomena and the socioeconomic influences circumscribing their lives. Natural disasters, unexpected deaths, and continued racist oppression serve as bitter reminders of the near-tragic dimensions of life, for to be black in America is to experience calamity as an ever-present reality, to live on the brink of apocalypse.

Although the apocalypse looms large in *Sula*—in modern America with its world wars, in the topsy-turvy world of the Bottom—the end of the world has already occurred and will be repeated to a greater or lesser degree in the future.[1] The omniscient narrator's account of the community's ironic genesis as part of a "nigger joke" is as much an end as it is a beginning:

> A good white farmer promised freedom and a piece of bottom land to his slave if he would perform some very difficult chores. When the slave completed the work, he asked the farmer to keep his end of the bargain. Freedom was easy—the farmer had no objection to that. But he didn't want to give up any land. So he told the slave that he was very sorry that he had to give him valley land. He had hoped to give a him a piece of the Bottom. The slave blinked and said he thought valley land was bottom land. The master said, "Oh, no! See those hills? That's bottom land, rich and fertile."
>
> "But it's high up in the hills," said the slave.
>
> "High up from us," said the master, "but when God looks down, it's the bottom. That's why we call it so. It's the bottom of heaven—best land there is."
>
> So the slave pressed his master to try to get him some. He preferred it to the valley. And it was done. The nigger got the hilly land, where planting was backbreaking, where the soil slid down and washed away the seeds, and where the wind lingered all through the winter.
>
> Which accounted for the fact that white people live on the rich valley floor in that little river town in Ohio, and the blacks populated the hills above it, taking small consolation in the fact that every day they could literally look down on the white folks.[2]

The narrator's story of how the Bottom comes into existence recalls the etiological animal tale with its account of the events taking place in the fabled time of "beginnings." Such accounts often involve the acts of supernatural beings or heroes and heroines of larger-than-life stature. Frequently there is a contest that pits God or the devil against a lesser adversary who is bested in a duel of wit or strength. Tales of origins (like "How God Made the Butterflies" or "Never Seen His Equal") have much to do with social inequities and serve a didactic purpose in explaining social or natural phenomena. One of the lessons which the story of the Bottom's origin imparts is relevant to the role that language plays in the black experience. The white farmer, like Adam in Genesis, is godlike in his ability to determine the destiny of the black slave and his descendants. Naïveté proves to be the slave's downfall, for he readily accepts the version of reality the white farmer calls into being through the spoken word. Thus, even after Emancipation the slave becomes the butt of the joke as he is confined to a toilsome existence not far removed from slavery. Yet the dynamics of the master-slave relationship that is so often the focus in the folktales is not without its inherent surprises and reversals, as Trudier Harris observes (Fiction and Folklore 52–71). The slave and his descendants who are forced to live in the Bottom demonstrate their pluck and mettle in an uncertain modern world by their efforts at transforming their day-to-day circumstances.

Among those in the Bottom there is the attempt to turn the tables on the white power structure responsible for the chaos that those in the community experience. The resounding laughter which valley residents hear emanating from the Bottom is self-reflexive, cathartic, as it becomes an integral part of the pain of black life in white America. That laughter stems from the sheer survival capabilities of the folk, their ability to persevere in the most difficult of circumstances. When Sula returns after a mysterious ten-year absence, Nel, who has failed to establish meaningful ties with anyone in the community, welcomes the "rib-scraping laughter" she and Sula share in place of the "miscellaneous giggles" that mark her other relationships (85). The story of the Bottom's beginnings is laced with as much laughter as pain, and each time the story is told, not only is there a ritual reenactment of the cyclic oppression of black life, but an ironic awareness of the ability to transcend the problems of life through what Ellison calls "a sheer toughness of spirit" (Shadow and Act 94).

Oppression is constant in the characters' lives—in where they live, in their economic situation—and their past, present, and future form a continuity in the cycle of frustration from which the townsfolk cannot easily escape. The world view among those in the Bottom therefore challenges the notion of attaining freedom in a remote heaven, and the community discovers that they must cope with the injustices of life, not by a naive faith in a futuristic reward, but by an affirmation of the strength and endurance emanating from the past.

Folk creations such as the cakewalk and the black bottom, emphasis on the importance of dreams, omens, and rituals, and especially, the townsfolks' attitude toward death, indicate vestiges of a culturally vibrant West African heritage at odds with a Judeo-Christian mythological system. The narrative is structured around Shadrack's National Suicide Day, one of many ritualistic events whose purpose is containing the disorder that so freely pervades the characters' lives, and Shadrack's appearance at the beginning, middle, and end of the novel could well be considered Morrison's attempt to satisfy the demand for fictive order. Shadrack, ravaged by the events of World War One, is the archetypal displaced modern American: "Twenty-two years old, weak, hot, frightened, not daring to acknowledge the fact that he didn't even know who or what he was . . . with no past, no language, no tribe, no source, no address book, no comb, no pencil, no clock, no pocket handkerchief, no rug, no bed, no can opener, no faded postcard, no soap, no key, no tobacco pouch, no soiled underwear and nothing nothing nothing to do" (10).

The shell-shocked war veteran serves as priest and prophet to the Bottom, exorcising the townsfolk of their misery while heralding their inevitable day of doom. He is identified with John the Baptist: "His eyes were so wild, his hair so long and matted, his voice was so full of authority and thunder that he caused panic on the first, or Charter, National Suicide Day in 1920" (12). Community lore also associates him with Christ: "Then Reverend Deal took it up, saying the same folks who had sense enough to avoid Shadrack's call were the ones who insisted on drinking themselves to death or womanizing themselves to death. 'May's well go on with Shad and save the Lamb the trouble of redemption'" (13–14). Ostensibly, Shadrack's presence represents the community's imminent attainment of order and progress, but the reality of his life belies that expectation. Madness has rendered Shadrack incapable of redeeming anyone, including himself. Instead, the tunnel, the cherished symbol of progress, collapses while Shadrack, the maddened priest-prophet, stands at a distance ringing his death bell.

Shadrack's tragicomic holiday fails to end the community's constant disorder. Deaths steeped in imagery of fire and water interrupt the rhythm of life in the Bottom, and each one of these deaths, except Sula's, is both bizarre and unexpected. Catastrophic events such as these not only reveal the absurdity of the community's endeavors to attain an Edenic existence within the context of Western history, but also serve as a commentary on the futility of Morrison's efforts to create an orderly fictional world whose setting is in modern America. A gesture equally as unavailing is the attempt to curtail the plague of robins, one of many omens accompanying Sula's disruptive return to the Bottom. The presence of evil in all of its subtle manifestations is an altogether inescapable part of African-American life.

Perhaps more important to an understanding of Morrison's fictive apocalypse, however, are the similarities between Shadrack's annual ritual and the celebration of the end of the world among many non-Western cultures whose conception of time is circular, not linear. The end of the world is believed to have already occurred. Subsequent annual celebrations of this past even provide a link between what Mircea Eliade refers to as the sacred, primordial time of a community's "beginnings" and its present sociopolitical conditions (54–55). Considered in this larger, mythic context, the recurrence of Shadrack's National Suicide Day, with its accompanying ritualistic emotional display, is reminiscent of the community's vibrant cultural past. The event offers a necessary buffer against the onslaught of history and, therefore, reveals a continuity between the Bottom's past, present, and future that is both redemptive and psychologically gratifying. In the Bottom, then, the negative effects of time can be overcome.

Eva's troublesome dreams in which Plum tries to reenter her womb also have mythic implications: They reveal the latent impulse to recover the psychological wholeness characteristic of black life prior to slavery. As living proof of the damage that slavery and its aftermath have wrought upon the male psyche, the male characters in the novel are, like Plum, very much in need of the heroic stature that might well have been theirs in the community's mythic past. Eva's wandering husband Boy Boy, for example, can never settle down long enough to accept the responsibilities associated with manhood; Tar Baby, a half-white hillbilly, is the town drunk; the Deweys are destined to remain homogenous children; Ajax is unable to fulfill his desires for flight and must watch airplanes from ground level; and Jude, Nel's unfaithful husband, considers marriage to be the only means by which he can validate his questionable manhood. These men are all scarcely shadows of their true selves, figuratively emasculated by a society whose tokens of manhood—wealth, prestige, and political power—are reserved for whites only.

Appropriately enough, it is Eva, the larger-than-life matriarch of the Peace family, who offers a vital historical connection with the past. Her indomitable strength, the resourcefulness that prompts her to sacrifice her leg in an effort to provide for her family, and the survival capabilities which allow her to overcome numerous tragedies all make her a timeless character whose influence in the community is boundless. Sula rejects the community's vibrant past when she places her grandmother Eva in a rest home— an abominable act which precipitates the later cosmic disharmony in the Bottom.

Eva is a stabilizing force, and one of the distinctive features of African-American writing is the presence of ancestors like Eve who, as Morrison puts it, "are sort of timeless people whose relationships to the characters are benevolent, instructive, and protective, and they provide a certain kind of wisdom" ("Rootedness: The Ancestor as Foundation" 343). Eva's is an ancient wisdom extending far beyond the mother wit that allows her to support three young children without either the financial or emotional support of her elusive husband. Hers is spiritual knowledge, omniscience. Before Hannah's startling death, Eva dreams of a red wedding dress. And although she is not present at Chicken Little's drowning, she recounts the circumstances surrounding this tragic event with amazing accuracy. She is an Eve figure in an upside-down Eden, the mother, creator of life, who, paradoxically, chooses to sacrifice Plum's life in order to preserve his damaged manhood. Plum's death is quite a victory. Armed with her mythic consciousness, Eva no doubt realizes that death is tantamount to a return to the womb, so she willingly ignites the flames releasing Plum from his tortured existence and allowing him to return to an eternal past.[3]

In the community's collective unconscious, then, the apocalypse, an event prefigured by the many deaths and disasters, endings and beginnings, is indeed a hopeful affair signaling the recovery of a lost past—much like Marcus Garvey's idealized Africa—characterized by freedom, vitality, and psychological wholeness. The novel emphasizes with forceful clarity that, although the white world may become extinct, the black world will not. It cannot. Those in the Bottom are fully aware of their marginal status in a racially divided country and that their dignity as a people depends on the destruction of a society hostile to the black sense of self.

Female Bonding and the Quest for Wholeness

In her fictionalization of the apocalypse and its implications for twentieth-century black America, Morrison delves deeply into the particular problems confronting African-American women. The relationship between Nel Wright and Sula Peace, whose bond is suggestive of the wholeness characteristic of life prior to the disruptive effects of slavery and capitalism, directs attention to the limitations society imposes.[4] Marriage, family, and the pursuit of middle-class standards of success all prove unfulfilling for Nel, who assumes the traditional roles the community prescribes and retains her social identity, though her personal identity is nonexistent. Sula, by contrast, is a free-spirited woman whose determination to define herself places her at odds with the culturally rich community. Hers is the dilemma of one out of touch with the historic black past. In their search for wholeness, both women find their world rife with contradictions and tensions, and they experience a profound sense of alienation in a world that evolves no terms for their existence.

Nel and Sula's relationship offers temporary escape from the tensions inherent in the community's patriarchal structure, however. As outsiders, they find in female bonding the wholeness society inhibits:

> Because each had discovered years before that they were neither white nor male, and that all freedom and triumph was forbidden to them, they had set about creating something else to be. Their meeting was fortunate, for it let them use each other to grow on. Daughters of distant mothers and incomprehensible fathers (Sula's because he was dead; Nel's because he wasn't), they found in each other's eyes the intimacy they were looking for. (44–45)

Their early, unbroken relationship is highlighted in the pivotal chapter "1922," which begins in the spring when the girls are twelve years old, discovering both each other and the world around them. Cleverly, and consistent with the emphasis which mythic cultures place on natural phenomena as a reflection of human affairs, Morrison interweaves with their coming of age imagery suggestive of maturity in the natural world and underscores the irony of their romantic hopes for fulfillment as black women in modern America. In the Bottom's temporal universe sunflowers weep, irises curl and turn brown, the maturity summer occasions precedes death: Chicken Little accidentally drowns after Sula swings him over a pond. One of many circular patterns in the narrative, the "closed place in the water" (87) figures both a beginning and an end, birth and death—the existential dilemma in which Nel and Sula are caught. Later, at the novel's ambiguous end, Nel's symbolic return to the past is prompted by her remembrance of this tragic incident.

Nel follows a historically prescribed path which leads her away from the freedom and vitality that are characteristic of her youth. Despite her early maternal disavowal, she becomes wife, mother, and good church woman— much like her mother Helene does. Early in the novel the reader is informed of Helene's questionable familial past and of her middle-class attempts to distance herself from her mother's "wild blood." Upon returning to the South, however, the beginnings of the black experience in this country, Helene is forced to confront the painful reality of black life: Medallion's paragon of middle-class respectability is insulted by a conductor who calls her "gal" as she attempts to walk through a "whites only" car of a Jim Crow train and she is later forced to relieve herself in the woods.

Helene's Edenic existence is immediately shattered, her defenses collapse, she turns to "custard." Her efforts at ordering her life through a traditional lifestyle prove as futile as those of her mother.

Only by bonding with Sula does Nel experience the "me-ness" she earlier affirms. When Sula returns to the Bottom after a ten-year absence, Nel "felt new, soft and new" (85). Hers is the beginning of a symbolic rebirth. Significantly, this rebirth is given fullest expression outside the context of traditional institutions such as marriage and the family—stifling institutions in which Nel has sought permanence.

Sula's journey toward self-determination places her at odds with pursuits that would limit her achievements. Hers is a circuitous quest for self that takes her outside the Bottom's narrow confines, then back to her beginnings, and as her rule-defying behavior reveals, she maintains fidelity to her declaration to make herself. She is a transcendent female character who, like the badman hero of folklore fame, is able to defy death. "When creating Sula, I had in mind a woman of force," Morrison says in an interview. "In a way she is distilled. She doesn't stop existing even after she dies. In fact, what she left behind is more powerful after she is dead than when she was alive" ("Complexity: Toni Morrison's Women" 254). African-American folklore includes accounts of reckless, defiant figures who live according to their own rules rather than by those society prescribes and die with a faint, wry smile. Sula is no less compelling an individual. Her illness brings Nel to her bedside for what is to be the final earthly confrontation between the two estranged best friends. In pain, suffering with a burning fever, as thin as a rail, Sula loses none of her wit or resolve. She is dying like a redwood, she informs Nel. Even at the point of death Sula proves that she is bigger than life: "Sula felt her face smiling. 'Well, I'll be damned,' she thought, 'it didn't even hurt. Wait'll I tell Nel'" (128).

In much the same way that Shadrack becomes a community demigod, Sula too finds that her rule-defying behavior earns her a place in community lore. The antics which make her ripe for inclusion in the town's gossip begin when she is still a youth. A group of bullies provide Sula an opportunity to show just how reckless and daring a woman can be. Sula's bravado in defense of her best friend Nel is noteworthy:

> Sula squatted down in the dirt road and put everything down on the ground: her lunchpail, her reader, her mittens, her slate. Holding the knife in her right hand, she pulled the slate toward her and pressed her left forefinger down hard on its edge. Her aim was determined but inaccurate. She slashed

off only the tip of her finger. The four boys stared open-mouthed at the wound and the scrap of flesh, like a button mushroom, curling in the cherry blood that ran into the corners of the slate.

Sula raised her eyes to them. Her voice was quiet. "If I can do that to myself, what you suppose I'll do to you?"

The shifting dirt was the only way Nel knew that they were moving away; she was looking at Sula's face, which seemed miles and miles away. (46–47)

At the same time that the reader feels compelled to criticize Sula because of her unorthodox actions, Morrison works to elicit admiration for the young woman who intimidates her would-be attackers.

In literature as well as in life, whenever women dare to move outside of socially prescribed roles, however, they tend to encounter opposition. Sula finds herself in this same kind of predicament when the townsfolk label her a witch because of her indifference to established conventions. She causes havoc among Eva's borders by interfering with the newly married couples and harassing the Deweys. It is her response to Hannah's tragic death that causes the most speculation concerning her true nature. Sula stands trans-fixed as Hannah burns to death, watching the incident without uttering a word. While the townsfolk suggest that she watches in shock, Eva hazards her own interpretation of Sula's actions: she watches because she is inter-ested.

Sula's unaccountable actions are a part of the mystical universe that dis-tinguishes the Bottom from Medallion, and the lore the community cre-ates regarding one of its two most notorious residents is just as intriguing as Sula's actions. Regarding Sula's alleged sexual escapades with white men, the townsfolk conjure images of what that kind of union would be like: "Every one of them imagined the scene, each according to his own predi-lections—Sula underneath some white man—and it filled them with chok-ing disgust" (98–99). Their fear of the feminine principle prompts them at one point to attribute her weird behavior to the menstrual cycle. Sula acts the way she does because of her "nature." She becomes the supreme embodiment of evil, a visible reminder of the way in which harmful influ-ences invade their otherwise uneventful lives. "The purpose of evil was to survive it," the omniscient narrator points out, "and they determined (with-out ever knowing they had made up their minds to do it) to survive floods, white people, tuberculosis, famine and ignorance" (78).

This same kind of ambiguity, perpetuated largely by word of mouth, follows Sula throughout her life. Her attempts to account for her activities during her ten-year absence from the Bottom does little to diffuse the mystery surrounding her character. Sula insists that she was away at college, but a formal education could hardly be expected to produce the confusion Sula sows. Nor could her disillusionment with men be solely responsible for her reckless behavior. Sula is both natural and supernatural—more than a mere woman—and represents a departure from the qualities that define Eva and Hannah. "Sula was distinctly different," the omniscient narrator explains. "Eva's arrogance and Hannah's self-indulgence merged in her and, with a twist that was all her own imagination, she lived out her days exploring her own thoughts and emotions, giving them full reign, feeling no obligation to please anybody unless their pleasure pleased her" (102).

Her self-reliant lifestyle begins with Chicken Little's accidental drowning and the trauma she suffers when she overhears Hannah's statement that she loved Sula but didn't like her. As a result of the emotional wounds she suffers, she turns inward and rejects society's dictates. She becomes one in a long line of characters in Morrison's canon who are dangerously free from the necessary sustenance the community provides. Sula atones for having refused the life-sustaining traditions and rituals of the Bottom by dying tragically and alone.

By far, the greatest and most formidable adversary that Sula takes on is the Bottom's prescriptive roles for women. Her bold, brassy, defiant manner prompts her to belch in public, attend church suppers without wearing underwear, and put her grandmother Eva in a rest home—all without any sign of remorse. She even goes so far as to sleep with the men in the community—including the husband of her best friend—and discard them when she tires of their presence. Serious commitment to any one man is not a part of Sula's agenda; self-discovery is. When Eva urges her to mend her ways, marry and bear children, Sula's response is to the point: "I don't want to make somebody else. I want to make myself" (80). Marriage and family life requires, in Sula's estimation, the ultimate self-sacrifice—one that she is either unwilling or unable to make. So she chooses to live a life without any emotional attachments. She and Shadrack, the town outcasts, share a mutual understanding based largely on their indifference toward established conventions. Operating outside the realm of what the townsfolk call normal or appropriate, both are labeled devils.

Sula remains enshrouded in mystery. Those in the Bottom feel that she has been marked from birth. Her curious birthmark which grows darker through the years sets her apart from the rest of the townsfolk. Each individual sees in that birthmark something different. The omniscient narrator describes it as a stemmed rose. Jude thinks that it resembles a rattlesnake. After having witnessed firsthand Sula's reckless behavior, the community asserts that the mysterious birthmark is Hannah's ashes. Whatever special endowments Sula possesses are to be attributed to the townsfolk's vivid imaginations exacerbated by their fear of the unknown, however, and their humorous attempts at counter conjure are revealing of their own fear of women who dare to step outside of socially prescribed roles.

Sula's estrangement from the community is measured in terms of her exploration of her psychological chaos. Unable to find fulfillment either in the Bottom or in the larger society, having lost Nel, "the closest thing to both an other and a self," Sula turns inward (103). And the natural world—the peculiar quality of May, the plague of robins—mirrors the societal disorder that has helped create Morrison's enigmatic protagonist.

A Pilgrimage to the Origins

Paradoxically, although Sula sows discord in the Bottom with her rule-defying behavior, she has a close affinity with the community's mythic past. Ajax is drawn to her because she reminds him of his conjure woman-mother. The townsfolk consider Sula a devil and attempt to ward off her evil by placing broomsticks across their steps and sprinkling salt on their doorsteps. Sula becomes the personification of the evil that pervades their lives. As a result of her presence, the community fortifies itself against her. "They began to cherish their husbands and wives, protect their children, repair their homes and in general band together against the devil in their midst" (102). With Sula present, the Bottom's communal bond is strengthened. Bonnie Barthold's comments on the novel are revealing of the effects of Sula's unaccountable behavior: "if Sula conjures with evil, she is also a means, however ironic, toward both goodness and truth. And in the events that follow her death, there is a similarly ambiguous suggestion of her power over time. It is as though her death mythically triggers a temporal chaos that, living, she had kept at bay, a disaster that is catastrophic for the Bottom" (110–11).

Sula uses sex as a means of exploring herself, of commemorating her estrangement from time. Her private reminiscences after one of many such encounters with Ajax indicate that she is a creative artist, a blues singer or a sculptor perhaps, whose artistic enterprises have led her back to a germinal mode of matter:

"There aren't any more new songs and I have sung all the ones there are. I have sung them all. I have sung all the songs there are." She lay down again on the bed and sang a little wandering tune made up of the words *I have sung all the songs all the songs I have sung all the songs there are* until, touched by her own lullaby, she grew drowsy, and in the hollow of near sleep she tasted the acridness of gold, left the chill of alabaster and smelled the dark, sweet stench of loam. (118)

Sula's death is a rite of passage by which she recovers the community's ancestral past. Alone, alienated from the Bottom, having explored herself freely, she assumes a fetal position and descends through water and darkness. Hers is a successful ritualistic return to the "beginnings":

It would be here, only here, held by this blind window high above the elm tree, that she might draw her legs up to her chest, close her eyes, put her thumb in her mouth and float over and down the tunnels, just missing the dark walls, down, down until she met a rain scent and would know the water was near, and she would curl into its heavy softness and it would envelop her, carry her, and wash her tired flesh always. Always. Who said that? She tried hard to think. Who was it that had promised her a sleep of water always? The effort to recall was too great; it loosened a knot in her chest that turned her thoughts again to the pain. (128)

The imagery Morrison uses in describing Sula's death is reminiscent of that used to describe Chicken Little's drowning, Eva's dream of Plum's return to her womb, and the community's march to the mouth of the tunnel at the novel's climactic end. Each of these events suggests a possible return to the womb, the beginnings of life, and reveals an awareness of an alternative reality distinct from that of the West. Although they are victimized by a world that is indifferent and, more often, hostile to their aspirations, Morrison's characters are able to draw upon their vast folk resources, move outside of history, and find a rare kind of survival power. Sula's reckless behavior notwithstanding, the Bottom's mythic past is viable and readily accessible.

The ultimate reversal taking place in narrative action thus involves a change in the Bottom's futuristic outlook. Following Sula's death many of the townsfolk who still cling to the belief in the possibility of attaining freedom in modern America feel "a brighter day was dawning" (129). They consider the prospect of employment in the building of the tunnel and the construction of a rest home—one accessible to blacks—signs of progress.

Their hopes are dashed when disturbances in the natural world signal an impending apocalypse. As fall ends, the community notices an unsettling change in the atmosphere and begins "wondering all the while if the world were coming to an end" (130). The seasons are awry: there is an unusually warm winter followed by a sudden freeze. Many of the townsfolk become ill and cannot work. Because of the sudden freeze, the crops fail, a major catastrophe for the small agricultural community. Theirs is "the beginning of trouble, that self-fulfilled prophecy that Shadrack carried on his tongue" (131). And without Sula to inspire them to solidarity, the townsfolk lose their motive for banding together and revert to their lax ways. The social and economic disorder the community seeks to contain remains an ever-present reality, despite their efforts at order and progress.

Eva, the clairvoyant ancestor, initiates Nel's pilgrimage to the origins by pointing out the oneness between Nel and Sula. In much the same way that Sula's callousness prompts her to watch her mother Hannah burn to death, Nel's indifference causes her to watch Chicken Little drown and keep secret the details of his tragic death. Nel recognizes that it has been Sula, not Jude, who has allowed her to explore herself freely. The imagery in the closing scene emphasizes a recovery of circular cosmic time. Like the mythical ancestor, the community's guardian whose presence remains constant, even after death, Sula transcends the grave, is finally one with the natural world, and establishes a continuity between past and present, temporal and eternal, natural and supernatural. "Shall We Gather at the River," the gospel song which the townsfolk intone at Sula's funeral, is an ironic one in this context (149). It refers not to the Jordan River which prefigures life in heaven, but to the river in which Chicken Little drowns and the Eden of Nel and Sula's early, unbroken relationship. Sula has escaped the fallen modern world, returned to the past, and is now whole. Nel's cry, "a fine cry—loud and long—with circles of sorrow" (149), is suggestive of the self-knowledge attainable only through an affirmation of the past. At the close of the text, Nel, like Sula, transcends history and returns to a realm in which relationships are integrated, not fragmented.

Both Nel and Sula, whose complementary relationship embodies the vitality of a mythic past, then, successfully enact the pilgrimage to the origins. For Sula, death is the last trial the individual must undergo before attaining life. Death is the tragic end that allows another beginning. Nel is just beginning this journey at the novel's end. As she contemplates the significance of her relationship with Sula, she attains psychological wholeness. Her remembrance of the past serves as catalyst for her moment of renewal and the recovery of the "always" that Shadrack's ritual is intended to bring.

At the novel's end the Bottom has collapsed. Shadrack, the insane prophet of doom, is without a congregation. In Morrison's fictional universe, though, the apocalypse gives way, not to Revelation's new heaven and earth, but to a community of partially dispossessed women who forge a sense of self based on the impulse to reconstruct the broken black historical continuum.

CHAPTER **7** Gloria Naylor, The Women of Brewster Place

> *It would be fatal for the nation to overlook the urgency of the moment and to
> underestimate the determination of the Negro. This sweltering summer of the
> Negro's legitimate discontent will not pass until there is an invigorating
> autumn of freedom and equality. 1963 is not an end, but a beginning. Those
> who hope that the Negro needed to blow off steam and will now be content will
> have a rude awakening if the Nation returns to business as usual. There will be
> neither rest nor tranquillity in America until the Negro is granted his
> citizenship rights. The whirlwinds of revolt will continue to shake the
> foundations of our nation until the bright day of justice emerges.*
> Martin Luther King Jr., "I Have a Dream" speech

In her first novel, The Women of Brewster Place, Gloria Naylor searches for an
authorial voice with which to tell or rather retell the stories of partially
dispossessed women. Narrative action is thus grounded in a specifically
cultured and gendered context in which voice and all of its associations is
directed toward subverting the forms of authority patriarchy legitimizes
and scripting a new world order among women of color. The apocalypse,
an event figured by the dismantling of the brick wall at the novel's end,
occurs as a result of the efforts on the part of politically conscious women
and results in an expansion of their sphere of influence.

Brewster Place: The Making of an Urban Folk Community

Gloria Naylor furthers the story of apocalypse in the African-American tradition with her fictional accounts of partially dispossessed women who,
despite the abuses they suffer, manage somehow to keep keeping on. The
Women of Brewster Place, the first in a series of four novels, speaks of the triumph of the human spirit over adversity and the role that sociopolitical
events play in helping to forge the collective consciousness necessary for
positive change. A series of rather unexpected reversals lands the seven

women, whose lives Naylor so vividly chronicles, on Brewster, a dilapidated housing project that is a breeding ground for hopelessness, poverty, and despair. Residency on Brewster is similar to one's having passed through the last phase of a grueling initiation rite in which the initiate is forced to surrender what is most dear. For Mattie, it is the security of home ownership; for Etta Mae, the prospect of social legitimacy, stability, and companionship in marriage; and for the lesbians Theresa and Lorraine, it is a more comfortable living space far removed from Brewster's squalid environs. In a very real sense, arrival on Brewster represents the end of the road for those whose dreams are indefinitely deferred. Once there, the residents are left to cope with their day-to-day circumstances as best they can.

In giving attention to the daily routine which characterizes life on Brewster, Naylor explores the practices and beliefs that helped to sustain the black folk community during slavery and its aftermath. Narrative emphasis on cooking, cleaning, or even nurturing reveals Brewster as much more than just a physical or geographic place; it is a symbolic reality far removed from a white, patriarchal space. Women serve as bearers of culture and tradition, or what Marjorie Pryse discusses as the power of conjure, even as they accommodate themselves to life in a decidedly urban locale (1–22). In an interview, Naylor mentions the women characters who appeared out of nothing and served as muses as she wrote, offering her guidance and direction ("A Conversation" 586). At least three residents of the community—Ben, Etta Mae, and Mattie—are transplanted southerners whose journey north suggests the viability of a rural folk tradition in an urban setting. Only by forming bonds among themselves do the women overcome life's difficulties and find the necessary strength to survive in a changing world. Not only that, but they also succeed at perpetuating the culture that supports the race. Naylor reminds the reader in the prologue "Dawn" that the novel is their story:

> Brewster Place became especially fond of its colored daughters as they milled like determined spirits among its decay, trying to make it a home. Nutmeg arms leaned over windowsills, gnarled ebony legs carried groceries up double flights of steps, and saffron hands strung out wet laundry on backyard lines. Their perspiration mingled with the steam from boiling pots of smoked pork greens, and it curled on the edges of the aroma of vinegar douches and Evening in Paris cologne that drifted through the street where they stood together—hands on hips, straight-backed, round-bellied, high-behinded women who threw their heads back when they laughed and exposed strong

teeth and dark gums. They cursed, badgered, worshipped, and shared their men. Their love drove them to fling dishcloths in someone else's kitchen to help them make the rent, or to fling hot lye to help him forget the bitch behind the counter at the five-and-dime. They were hard-edged, soft-centered, brutally demanding, and easily pleased, these women of Brewster Place.[1]

Among the many bonds the women establish, it is the mother-daughter relationship that proves to be crucial to restoring the social cohesion lost with the trek north. Mattie Michael, the first in a long line of central mother figures in Naylor's canon, plays a key role on Brewster with her strength and timeless wisdom. The road that leads Mattie to Brewster Place is a long and winding one indeed, and it begins with her sheltered childhood in Rock Vale, Tennessee. Mattie's naïveté makes her ripe for seduction by the smooth-talking Butch Fuller whose worldliness both repels and attracts Mattie. That she seems drawn to Butch suggests she both is and is not responsible for their sexual affair. Butch is a self-professed ladies' man who refuses to commit himself to any one woman. But Mattie finds him more appealing than the conservative Fred Watson, her father's hand-picked suitor. Mattie falls victim to the advances of Butch Fuller one spring afternoon in the country, choosing to name her son Basil because he is conceived in a field of herbs. Butch manages to escape the wrath of Sam Michael and, along with it, the responsibilities accompanying fatherhood, leaving Mattie to face her father's wrath and community reproach alone.

From the time that Mattie leaves home to her arrival on Brewster, she is caught in circumstances that are beyond her control. Fate, society, and lapses in judgment are catalysts for her residency on the dead-end street. Her thoughts as she leaves for the North indicate that there is a certain inevitability associated with the move: "She just wanted to lay her head on the cushioned seat and suspend time, pretend that she had been born that very moment on that very bus, and that this was all there was and ever would be. But just then the baby moved, and she put her hands on her stomach and knew that she was nurturing within her what had gone before and would come after. This child would tie her to that past and future as inextricably as it was now tied to her every heartbeat" (25). The kindly Miss Eva rescues Mattie and her young son from the streets and offers them the warmth, comfort, and security they need. Miss Eva's inquiries into Mattie's celibacy and devotion to Basil bring about a defensiveness on Mattie's part, however. Mattie's behavior, Miss Eva implies, is unnatural, and the young woman clings to Basil out of a sense of loneliness, preferring his love to that of a mature male companion.

There is some truth in Miss Eva's claims, for Mattie tries to compensate for the love she has been denied through sacrificing herself for her son. Regarding the mother-daughter that figures so prominently in the text, Larry Andrews notes that "One of the problems several women face is that in their isolation they come to focus all their needs on their children and define themselves exclusively as mothers, thus enacting a male-defined, exploitative role" (5). It is Mattie who is at least partly responsible for Basil's irresponsible behavior. In her efforts to protect him from the harsh realities of urban life, she succeeds at creating a man unable to accept the responsibilities of manhood: "Whatever was lacking within him that made it impossible to confront the difficulties of life could not be supplied with words. She saw it now. There was a void in his being that had been padded and cushioned over the years, and now that covering had grown impregnable. She bit on her bottom lip and swallowed back a sob. God had given her what she prayed for—a little boy who would always need her" (52). In rearing Basil Mattie exhibits a toxic love, and she atones for her mistake with Basil's abandonment of her and the loss of her home.

If Mattie's maternal devotion brings about the losses which result in her arrival on Brewster, it is this same devotion that proves to be liberating for the women in the novel. Naylor creates a community of women among whom the life-giving maternal bond has been ruptured and Mattie's presence allows a restoration of that bond. Nowhere is this more evident than in the relationship between Mattie and Ciel. Ciel is a grieving mother who has lost two children abruptly—one, through abortion; the other, through an accidental electrocution. Following the funeral for her daughter Serena, Ciel is in a death-in-life state. In what is surely the most moving scene in the novel, Mattie bathes Ciel carefully and tenderly, as a mother would. She then rocks her backward in time, symbolically back to the womb, thereby negating the psychologically destructive effects of temporality, the cycle that has led to the almost overwhelming tragedy Ciel now faces:

> Ciel moaned. Mattie rocked. Propelled by the sound, Mattie rocked her out of that bed, out of that room, into a blue vastness just underneath the sun and above time. She rocked her over Aegean seas so clean they shone like crystal, so clear the fresh blood of sacrificed babies torn from their mother's arms and given to Neptune could be seen like pink froth on the water. She

rocked her on and on, past Dachau, where soul-gutted Jewish mothers swept their children's entrails off laboratory floors. They flew past the spilled brains of Senegalese infants whose mothers had dashed them on the wooden sides of slave ships. And she rocked on.

She rocked her into her childhood and let her see murdered dreams. And she rocked her back, back into the womb, to the nadir of her hurt, and they found it—a slight silver splinter, embedded just below the surface of the skin. And Mattie rocked and pulled—and the splinter gave way, but its roots were deep, gigantic, ragged, and they tore up flesh with bits of fat and muscle tissue clinging to them. They left a huge hole, which was already starting to pus over, but Mattie was satisfied. It would heal. (104–5)

Ciel undergoes a mystical rebirth, not a repetition of the first, physical birth, but one that is spiritual in nature. Significantly, that birth takes place in private, outside the watchful gaze of a white, patriarchal society, and is oriented toward allowing her access to a new mode of existence in which she is no longer subject to the limitations imposed by time and space. The scene's reference to other bereaved mothers—those in Greek mythology, Jewish mothers during the holocaust, and Senegalese mothers—unites Mattie and Ciel with a broad community of dispossessed mothers who are denied the luxury of grief. In the patently unique community of women that is Brewster Place, Ciel grieves freely, however, and hers is a catharsis that is similar to the laughter that unites Mattie and Etta Mae. As if to reveal Ciel's new mode of existence, her narrative points toward new beginnings, concluding with a violation of the novel's rigid dawn-to-dusk temporal time frame: "And Ciel lay down and cried. But Mattie knew the tears would end. And she would sleep. And morning would come" (105).

Whether it is the mother wit that prompts Mattie to nurse Ciel back to life, or the timely advice on the ways of men she offers Etta Mae prior to the tryst with Reverend Woods, the maternal role is a key one on Brewster and it is one through which cultural values are transmitted. Kiswana Browne's mother penetrates the artificial identity her militant daughter assumes simply by drawing upon the resources of age, wisdom, and experience. A generational rift stemming from class as well as ideological differences separate the two women. Because of her identification with the black revolution, Kiswana feels compelled to reject her mother's conservative ideals in favor of a lifestyle that allows her to live and work among "my people." It takes a brief but pointed history lesson to force Kiswana into an awareness of the rich history she ignores in her pursuit of her radical goals. Mrs.

Browne tells of a lineage rooted in struggle: "My grandmother," Mrs. Browne began slowly in a whisper, "was a full-blooded Iroquois, and my grandfather a free black from a long line of journeymen who had lived in Connecticut since the establishment of the colonies. And my father was a Bajan who came to this country as a cabin boy on a merchant mariner" (86). She reminds Kiswana of the sacrifices she has made as a mother: "When I brought my babies home from the hospital, my ebony son and my golden daughter, I swore before whatever gods would listen—those of my mother's people or those of my father's people—that I would use everything I had and could ever get to see that my children were prepared to meet this world on its own terms, so that no one could sell them short and make them ashamed of what they were or how they looked—whatever they were or however they looked. And Melanie, that's not being white or red or black— that's being a mother."

Like the college-educated Dee in Alice Walker's "Everyday Use," Kiswana is a young woman whose sixties-based revolutionary ideals prompt her to deny her black folk heritage in favor of an identification with Mother Africa. Both Naylor and Walker offer narrative resolutions which privilege the ideology of the older generation over that of the overzealous youths who fail to appreciate the historic black struggle for freedom in this country, however, and the role that the folk have played in determining the course of history. Thus, Mrs. Browne's revelation of the strength and fortitude she inherits from her ancestors makes Kiswana appear phony and shallow—as artificial as the name she picks from an African dictionary.

The two women eventually discover that there are more commonalities between them than differences. Larry Andrews is correct when he asserts that Kiswana and her mother share a bond that is based upon sex (6). When she sees her mother approaching, Kiswana is careful to conceal the evidence of a live-in relationship with Abshu by hiding his shaving cream and razor in the bottom drawer of her dresser. Mrs. Browne is worried about the message Kiswana may be sending out as a result of her having a nude statuette in her living room, so she cautions her daughter about the vulnerabilities of single womanhood. But as the pair converse, Kiswana comes to recognize the fact that her mother is still a woman. The bright red nail polish Mrs. Browne wears is to appeal to the tastes of Mr. Browne, Kiswana's father. By the end of Kiswana's story, she and her middle-class mother share a spiritual oneness by virtue of their sexuality: "And she looked at the blushing woman on her couch and suddenly realized that her mother had trod through the same universe that she herself was now traveling.

Kiswana was breaking no new trails and would eventually end up just two feet away on that couch. She stared at the woman she had been and was to become" (87).

What unifies the otherwise disparate urban community of Brewster Place, then, is a shared sense of solidarity based on the challenges each faces in a white, patriarchal world. The brick wall separating Brewster from the larger society is symbolic of the marginalized space women are forced to occupy. It is outside of the social mainstream that the women experience what Gloria Wade-Gayles describes as "the distinguishing marks of black womanhood in white America" (3–4). The church is a central institution on Brewster, and Naylor's fictionalized representation of the religious discourse emanating from this underground institution lends credence to the narrator's assertion that "the people had their own language and music and codes" (2). Those who worship at the ironically named Canaan Baptist are the poor, the downtrodden, and the dispossessed—those for whom a belief in socioeconomic progress in urban America has proven false. Canaan's music and preaching reveals the essence of what Geneva Smitherman refers to as the sacred-secular continuum present in distinctly black modes of discourse, especially that emanating from the city (87–90). Lyrics from the well-known spiritual "Go Down Moses," once a popular code among repressed slaves, indicate a vital historic continuity between ancient Israel and contemporary urban black America and permeate Etta Mae's narrative: "Yes, my God is a mighty God / Lord, deliver / And he set old Israel free / Swallowed that Egyptian army / Lord, deliver / With the waves of the great Red Sea" (64).

Reverend Woods' sermon is an example of black oratory at its finest:

He glided to the podium with the effortlessness of a well-oiled machine and stood still for an interminable long moment. He eyed the congregation confidently. He only needed their attention for that split second because once he got it, he was going to wrap his voice around their souls and squeeze until they screamed to be relieved. They knew it was coming and waited expectantly, breathing in unison as one body. First he played with them and threw out fine silken threads that stroked their heart muscles ever so gently. They trembled ecstatically at the touch and invited more. The threads multiplied and entwined themselves solidly around the one pulsating organ they had become and tightened slightly, testing them for a reaction.

The "Amen, brothers" and "Yes, Jesus" were his permission to take that short hop from the heart to the soul and lay all pretense of gentleness aside.

Now he would have to push and pound with clenched fists in order to be felt, and he dared not stop the fierce rhythm of his voice until their replies had reached that fevered pitch of satisfaction. Yes, Lord—grind out the un-heated tenements! Merciful Jesus—shove aside the low-paying boss man. Perfect Father—fill me, fill me til there's no room, no room for nothing else, not even that great big world out there that exacts such a strange penalty for my being born black. (65)

One cannot help but discern the patently revolutionary consciousness which Woods' sermon creates in the responsive congregation. They are more concerned with a change in their present living conditions than with reach-ing heaven. That Naylor places the religious discourse of the church in Etta Mae's narrative is telling. It is through Etta Mae's blues-inspired perspective that the reader is best able to see the falsity of the Judeo-Christian ideals that Mattie espouses. There is no release from the loneliness and poverty the aging Etta Mae Johnson faces, and her attempts to lead Reverend Woods to the altar culminate in a disappointing one-night stand in a seedy motel room. Woods is a streetwise preacher, a charlatan who is concerned only about his material gain and his carnal lusts. The language Naylor uses to describe his sermon and its effect on the congregation anticipates the sexual union taking place between Woods and Etta Mae. After their brief affair is over, the only deliverance Etta Mae finds is through her sisterly bond with Mattie. Both women have experienced disappointment in love and it is in each other's company that they acquire the strength they both need.

The women's collective dream of freedom, given fullest expression in "The Block Party," is laced with the folk beliefs and practices which have supported the black community from its rural beginnings. Each woman is symbolically united with Lorraine, the black woman as victim, and dreams of the brutal rape and Ben's senseless murder. There is a vital oneness cre-ated among all the women on Brewster as a result of the vulnerabilities of black womanhood. The women choose to respond to the perceived evil of their intrusive dreams as best they can: by placing open Bibles near their beds. Such conjuring on their part suggests the reliance upon a belief sys-tem that, as Pryse notes, derives from an oral not a written source (10). Etta Mae suppresses the truth of her dream by seeing what number she can play off of it: "Now I know snakes is 436 and a blue Cadillac is 234, but I gotta look in my book to see what a wall is. What do ya play off a wall Mattie?" (180). Mattie's dream-nightmare prior to the long-awaited block party is the culminating event in the narrative, the ultimate expression of a night world of horror, frustration, and chaos. She awakens from her troubled sleep, understandably relieved that her dream is unreal. Etta Mae then informs the reader that "We're gonna have a party" (189).

Where the systems legitimized by patriarchy have failed to offer the women of Brewster Place new life, they turn inward, look to each other, and find strength in the timeless practices emanating from the folk past. By so doing, they defy the fate prescribed by the amorphous white power structure responsible for the creation of the failing community. "Dusk" is just as much of a beginning as it is an end. Even though Brewster is condemned, the women, the omniscient narrator tells the reader, "still wake up" (192). They move elsewhere and continue the rituals and practices that have long been a sustaining influence in black America.

To Tear Down the Wall: Revolutionaries and Dreamers

In her fictionalization of the lives of women, Naylor pays close attention to the impact of African-American women on matters of race and sex in the latter half of the twentieth century. The text chronicles the gradual awakening of the dispossessed masses to their full potential as political entities, and it does so largely through the account of Mattie's dream-nightmare involving the dismantling of the brick wall, an apocalyptic event framed within the context of the failed promises of democracy. Underlying Kiswana Browne's organizational efforts on behalf of the formation of a tenants' association is the awareness, deeply rooted in a distinctly black consciousness, that America's promises are false. They are at best pipe dreams and at worst nightmares. Living conditions on Brewster are abysmally poor, with crumbling plaster, arthritic cold, and vermin-infested garbage dumps. And C. C. Baker and his gang contribute to the criminal element present in the community. Those on Brewster are unwilling heirs to the legacy of powerlessness which the political leaders responsible for the creation of the community have bequeathed. No one fights on behalf of Brewster's rights, the narrator tells the reader regarding the decision to impose the wall isolating the residents from the rest of the city, and the residents must rely on themselves rather than on the system if they are to realize positive change.

Brewster's origin as a political act therefore challenges the validity of the utopian postwar new world order the city alderman scripts with his glowing address at the community's inception: "They applauded wildly as the smiling alderman smashed a bottle of champagne against the edge of one of the buildings. He could hardly be heard over the deafening cheers as he told them, with a tear in the corner of his eye, it was the least he could do to help make space for all their patriotic boys who were on the way home from the Great War" (1). That the community emerges in the immediate aftermath of the Second World War is significant in terms of an understanding of Naylor's obvious concern with the various movements in the modern and contemporary eras influencing women's lives, for it is World War Two that had a profound impact in shaping the evolving mindset of black America. "The war so raised the level of consciousness of blacks and women that it needed the national soil for the Civil Rights Movement of the fifties and sixties and the Black Power Movement of the seventies," Gloria Wade-Gayles writes, "as well as the Women's Liberation Movement of the sixties and seventies" (20).

A number of historic events figure into the narrator's account of Brewster's beginning in "Dawn," thereby creating the illusion of progress, equality, and upward socioeconomic mobility: world war, the WPA program, and Brown versus the Topeka Board of Education. Brewster's rapid decline underscores the irony inherent in the historical vision held by those in positions of power and authority, however. The community is designed to fail, and it does. It is part of a self-fulfilling prophecy.

Naylor's clever choice of Langston Hughes' poem "Harlem" as an epigraph highlights the lives of those for whom the dream—whether it is love, acceptance, or socioeconomic progress—is all too often indefinitely deferred: "What happens to a dream deferred? Does it dry up / like a raisin in the sun? / Or fester like a sore and then run? / Does it stink like rotten meat? / Or crust and sugar over / like a syrupy sweet? / Maybe it just sags like a heavy load. / Or does it explode?" A philosophical musing on the ontological state of deferred dreams, the poem closes with a pointed question which begs the issue of violence as a response to unfulfilled longings. Naylor's text is then a conscious rewriting of Hughes' poem and the kind of social unrest which no doubt inspired Hughes to write. Indeed, the tensions surrounding Kiswana's attempts to organize a rent strike in defiance of the "one man" who owns the run-down buildings recall those leading to the 1935 race riot erupting in Harlem.[2]

Kiswana, a product of the sixties, conforms quite easily to what Mary Helen Washington refers to in her discussion of Alice Walker's evolutionary treatment of black women as the emergent woman ("An Essay on Alice Walker" 145–48). Young, ambitious, politically active, she is heir to the achievements of a new order, thus signaling the transition of women from death to life, ending to beginning. Her efforts at mobilizing the residents are reminiscent of the attempts of Civil Rights Workers in the rural South to register black voters. Despite the opposition Kiswana faces, she remains undaunted, and the ambiguous tenants' association slogan, "Today Brewster—Tomorrow America," suggests the expanding sphere of influence on the part of politically conscious women of color. Together with her boyfriend Abshu, she lays the groundwork for a cultural awakening on Brewster based on an identification with Africa and its cultural artifacts.

More than any other story, it is Cora Lee's that shows the difficulties Brewster's two revolutionaries face when they try to bring about a change in the lives of those in the dormant community. Abshu, having secured a grant from the city, is to present a black production of Shakespeare's *A MidSummer Night's Dream*. Cora Lee's narrative begins with lines from the play: "True, I talk of dreams, / which are the children of an idle brain / Begot of nothing but vain fantasy" (107). The young woman is a high school drop out and single mother of seven. She leads a passive life consisting of a steady diet of soap operas and interruptions from her unruly children. Naylor stops short of casting Cora Lee into the role of the classic welfare mother by allowing the reader insight into the young woman's psychology. Cora Lee's preoccupation with motherhood is attributed to a childhood fixation on dolls. Her relationships with the men who father her children are seldom and short-lived. She remembers Sammy and Maybelline's father solely in terms of his gold-capped teeth and glass eye. Brucie's father promises to marry her, but leaves for a carton of milk and never returns. When the abuse she experiences in those relationships becomes too intense, she resigns herself to brief moments of sensual pleasure from the men who "show her the thing that felt good in the dark" (113). Up until the time Cora Lee attends the play, she is an anonymous ward of society, and her only acts of creation are the seven children she mothers then later neglects.

The dramatic transformation Cora Lee undergoes that evening indicates that Brewster is a place of magical rejuvenation, much like the enchanted forest in *Dream*.[3] Under the enchantment brought about by the prospect of attending the play, Cora Lee begins to envision a future that is radically different from the present. She is impressed by Kiswana's fancy jeans, silk blouse, and expensive perfume. She thinks of her sister who lives in the middle-class community of Linden Hills and her brother who has a post office job. Not only does she work tirelessly that evening at cleaning her home, she even mends her children's worn clothing. Cora Lee resolves to be a better mother by checking her children's homework and attending PTA meetings. Her dreams of progress and upward socioeconomic mobility lead her to cast her daughter Maybelline into the role of the eloquent fairy queen who says fine things while on stage. Her son Brucie sees Bottom and asks if he, too, will someday look like a dumb ass and she is embarrassed. While on the way home Sammy asks if Shakespeare was black. Cora Lee responds optimistically, "Not yet," feeling guilty that she had once beaten him for writing rhymes on her bathroom wall.

Cora Lee's trip back to her apartment that night shows the difficulties of sustaining the magical vision she has entertained. Abshu's production notwithstanding, she remains powerless to break the cycle of poverty in which she is trapped. She returns to her neat, orderly home, only to be greeted by another shadow who lets himself in with his own key. The lines from Dream with which her narrative closes therefore offer a grim feeling of finality, with her ideal world of middle-class life dissolving into nothing: "If we shadows have offended, / Think but this, and all is mended: / That you have but slumber'd here, / While these visions did appear. / And this weak and idle theme, / No more yeilding but a dream"(126).

That Cora Lee fails to find lasting empowerment through a renewed black consciousness which stems from an identification with Africa, its people, and its culture is disappointing. Africa and the nationalist consciousness it inspires for Abshu and Kiswana is not an alternative for Cora Lee. When she next appears, she is pregnant again and among those present at the dream-fantasy block party.

It is Mattie Michael, Brewster's central mother-figure, who dreams the women's communal dream of freedom. The bickering and infighting which plagues the community as it attempts to mobilize against the white power structure gives way, in the community's collective unconscious, to a unified effort designed to bring about light and enlightenment. Mattie's dream is what Northrup Frye calls demonic, with its dystopic imagery suggestive of impending doom and destruction: there is a torrential rain storm, blood on the wall, and blaring police sirens (The Anatomy of Criticism 40–41). The men are noticeably absent in the reality Naylor inscribes; only women are present during what seems to be a ritual cleansing of the universe from the guilt over Lorraine's rape and Ben's murder. Ciel returns to Mattie, her surrogate mother, in a brief reunion between the two women. Amidst a fresh downpour, the women proceed to dismantle the wall: "The blunt-edged whoop of the police sirens could be heard ramming through the traffic on its way to Brewster Place. Theresa flung her umbrella away so she could have both hands free to help the other women who were now bringing her bricks. Suddenly, the rain exploded around their feet in a fresh downpour, and the cold waters beat on the top of their heads—almost in perfect unison with the beating of their hearts" (188).

Even though Brewster is condemned, the women continue to dream. They persevere in the face of seemingly overwhelming odds. Armed with only the remnants of their aspirations, the women move elsewhere and start life anew. Their dreams remain inviolable; they "ebb and flow, ebb and flow, but never disappear" (192).

Women, Multivocality, and the New World Order

The primary relationships with which Naylor is concerned exist among partially dispossessed women across time and space who are unified by the desire for a place where each is allowed just to be. Sometimes social circumstances work against their attaining their desired end, as with the lesbian bond between Lorraine and Theresa. In treating the very sensitive issue of lesbianism, Naylor chooses to focus on the community's response to the nontraditional lifestyle the women have chosen.[4] Mattie's assertion that the love the lesbians share is no different from what she has felt for other women does little to alleviate Brewster's insistent homophobia; nor does it rescue the two women from the fracturing of their relationship. Rape and madness await a newly assertive Lorraine when she tries to establish an identity apart from her submissive role with Theresa. Somehow both internal and external pressures prevent the two women from finding, on Brewster, the refuge each one seeks.

But Naylor suggests that harmonious relationships between women are not only possible but vital in ushering in the new world order. Her emotional energy was spent on creating a woman's world, she says in an interview, "because I knew it hadn't been done enough in literature" ("A Conversation" 579). Much of that woman-centered reality revolves around the use of oral tradition in the redefinition of self and society. Abena Busia notes that a distinguishing feature of contemporary black women's novels is the creation of a female narrator who can tell her own story ("Words Whispered Over Voids" 3). Each of the seven women in the text speaks in a voice that is at once both individual and communal, thereby resisting the univocal, authoritative closure which the novel's dawn-to-dusk narrative structure implies. Naylor's goal as creator and sovereign of the new fictive cosmology toward which the novel moves is to establish unity between the widely disparate voices of women, not just within but outside the text. Indeed, in her discussion of the responsive strategy of black women's narratives, Karla Holloway refers to the technique as being "a collective 'speaking out' of all the voices gathered within the text, authorial, narrative, and even the implicated reader" (*Moorings and Metaphors* 11). Mattie and Etta Mae are united by a coded laughter that "drew them into a conspiratorial circle against all the Simeons outside of that dead-end street, and it didn't stop until they were both weak from the tears that flowed down their faces" (61). As Mattie nurses the grieving Ciel back to life following the funeral for Serena, the sound of Ciel's primal moan propels the two women into space, establishing a vital oneness with dispossessed mothers across the diaspora. The brick wall symbolizes an imposed reality, but the voices of women transcend all artificially imposed constructs established by patriarchy. The result of this transcendence is a text that is multivocal and more closely reflects the realities faced by women, regardless of their time and place.[5]

In many respects, the novel, which consists of a community of seven different stories, is a conscious telling and retelling of the same story, with the search for an appropriate ending.[6] Naylor mentions her fear of narrative endings and the grim sense of finality which the completion of *Brewster Place* conveyed. She compares the bound copy of the novel to a tombstone ("A Conversation" 586). Before finishing the novel she had already begun the emotional trek to her second novel, *Linden Hills,* whose environs are visible from Brewster. Oral tradition, or the narrative art of storytelling pervasive in her canon, allows Naylor to subvert the closure she fears and continue her story without interruption. Far from signaling an end, then, the personal crises her female characters experience give way to a new beginning—one which mirrors the new world order Naylor conjures into existence by the spoken word.

The ebony phoenix symbolizes the woman as narrator: each storyteller emerges out of the ashes of personal catastrophe. Ciel finds new life in the wake of her losses. Morning heralds another beginning for Ciel. In "The Block Party," a story with multiple authorship, she has a good job in San Francisco working in an insurance company and is in a relationship with another man. The light, love, and laughter that greet Etta Mae as she ascends the stairs after her tryst with Woods reverse the darkness and dejection she feels when he leaves her. The women enjoy a life-giving relationship that allows them to triumph over tragedy.

The ending of the text, with its account of the women's attempt to dismantle the brick wall, scripts the dawning of a new day. Together, the women challenge the restrictions of the amorphous white male political system responsible for Brewster's creation. No longer bound by patriarchy and its authoritarian mandates, the women defy the fate to which they have been consigned. Theirs is a movement away from a scriptocentric reality with its fixed boundaries and toward a cosmological system that is oral, female, and collective.

NOTES

Introduction

1. A number of scholars who have investigated the apocalypse in the American literary tradition include a discussion of the African-American novel within the larger context of the American novel and its archetypes. See Robinson, *American Apocalypses*; R. W. B. Lewis, *Trials of the Word*; and May, *Toward a New Earth*.

2. Smitherman is among the first linguists to devote attention to a formal analysis of black language structures. She refers to the religious practice of testifying, which entails one's giving public witness concerning God's benevolence. See *Talkin' and Testifyin'*, 8–22.

3. I am indebted to the following sources for an understanding of the history surrounding the production of apocalypse and its religious and secular manifestations: Russell, *Apocalyptic: Ancient and Modern*; Charles, *Studies in the Apocalypse*; and R. W. B. Lewis, *Trials of the Word*, 184–235.

4. Blassingame, *The Slave Community*; Herskovitz, *The Myth of the Negro Past*; Levine, *Black Culture and Black Consciousness*; and Raboteau, *Slave Religion*.

5. Cone discusses the double meaning associated with the conception of heaven among African Americans in *The Spirituals and the Blues*, 86–107. Fisher's discussion of this concept is grounded in his study of the spirituals as "oral historical documents." See *Negro Slave Songs in the United States*, 111–32.

6. Cone, *The Spirituals and the Blues*, 106. The most complete statement of Cone's theological views appears in *Black Theology and Black Power*.

7. Moses, *Black Messiahs and Uncle Toms*, and Howard-Pitney, *The Afro-American Jeremiad*.

Chapter One: Charles Chesnutt, *The Marrow of Tradition*

1. Chesnutt, *The Marrow of Tradition*, 7. Subsequent references to the novel are noted parenthetically in the text.

2. Andrews discusses the genesis of the novel in *The Literary Career of Charles W. Chesnutt*, 124–27. Render's account of the novel's genesis is less detailed but informative in *Charles W. Chesnutt*, 39–41.

3. Dance, *Shuckin' and Jivin*, 224–25. For other discussions of the "bad nigger," see Brearly, "Ba-ad Nigger," in *Mother Wit from the Laughing Barrel*, 578–85; Roberts, *From Trickster to Badman*, 171–215; and Thomas, *From Folklore to Fiction*, 43–79.

4. Chesnutt's characterization of the badman hero reflects, among other things, his middle-class bias and is in conflict with many of the traits Brearly assigns to the folk figure. Brearly makes quite a few controversial assertions regarding the badman. For insight into those assertions, see Dundes' editorial comments in "Ba-ad Nigger," *Mother Wit From the Laughing Barrel*, 578–79.

5. Brearly asserts that many "bad nigger" types confine their bravado to members of their own race, "Ba-ad Nigger," 583.

6. For insight into the controversy between Chesnutt and Washington, see H. M. Chesnutt, *Charles Waddell Chesnutt*, 170–82.

7. Bell mentions Chesnutt's use of an ironic voice in the characterization of Mammy Jane. See *The Afro-American Novel and Its Tradition*, 63–70.

8. H. M. Chesnutt offers an overview of the novel's lukewarm critical reception in *Charles Waddell Chesnutt*, 176–78.

Chapter Two: Richard Wright, *Native Son*

1. Wright, "How Bigger Was Born," *Native Son*, xxi. Subsequent references to the novel are noted parenthetically in the text.

2. Nagel discusses the novel's blindness motif in "Images of 'Vision' in *Native Son*," 151–80.

3. For folkloric accounts of flight, see Dorson, *American Negro Folktales*, and Abrahams, *Afro-American Folktales*.

4. I am indebted to Singh for an understanding of Wright's political ideology and attitude toward religion. See "Some Basic Ideas and Ideals in Richard Wright's Fiction," 78–84, and "Christian Heroes and Anti-Heroes in Richard Wright's Fiction," 90–104.

5. Kinnamon discusses the novel's color symbolism in *The Emergence of Richard Wright*, 135–36.

6. Both Singh and Kinnamon suggest that Wright intends Bigger to be a type of Christ.

Chapter Three: Ralph Ellison, *Invisible Man*

1. Ellison, *Invisible Man*, 493. Subsequent references to the novel are noted parenthetically in the text.

2. O'Meally offers a thorough investigation of the novel's folk forms in *The Craft of Ralph Ellison*, 78–104.

3. Roberts traces the trickster tradition in African-American culture to its African origins and explores the dynamics of the survival strategies the figure practices in *From Trickster to Badman*, 17–61. Thomas discusses Ellison's use of the trickster figure in *From Folklore to Fiction*, 92–99.

4. Gates suggests repetition and revision as fundamental to forms of black creative expression in *The Signifying Monkey*, xi–xxviii.

5. Horowitz discusses Ellison's use of the Brer Rabbit motif in a groundbreaking essay. See "Ralph Ellison's Modern Version of Brer Bear and Brer Rabbit in *Invisible Man*," 21–27.

Chapter Four: James Baldwin, *Go Tell it on the Mountain*

1. See Howe, "James Baldwin: At Ease in Apocalypse," 96–108.

2. Baldwin describes his conversion experience in detail in *The Fire Next Time*, 41–45.

3. Baldwin, *Go Tell It on the Mountain*, 16. Subsequent references to the novel are noted parenthetically in the text.

4. For insight into the literary, social, religious, and biographical significance of the father-son relationship in the text, I am indebted to Fabre, "Fathers and Sons in James Baldwin's *Go Tell It on the Mountain*," 120–38.

5. Allen discusses Baldwin's use of Scripture in "Religious Symbolism and Psychic Reality in Baldwin's *Go Tell It on the Mountain*," 166–86. O'Neale's essay, "Fathers, Gods, and Religion: Perceptions of Christianity and Ethnic Faith in James Baldwin," offers an insightful discussion of religion in Baldwin's texts, 125–41.

Chapter Five: LeRoi Jones [Imamu Amiri Baraka], *The System of Dante's Hell*

1. See criticisms of the novel in Littlejohn, *Black on White*, 96–100, and Margolies, *Native Sons*, 194–97.

2. LeRoi Jones, "Sound and Image," *The System of Dante's Hell*. Subsequent references to the novel are noted parenthetically in the text.

3. Brown discusses the text in terms of Jones' improvisation upon Dante in "LeRoi Jones [Imamu Amiri Baraka] as Novelist: Theme and Structure in *The System of Dante's Hell*," 132–42.

4. Jones outlines his philosophy regarding black art in *Blues People*, 1–16, and in *Home*, 105–15, 250–52.

5. Jones fully develops his ideas concerning a nonwhite community united by its victimization at the hands of an imperialist white power structure in *Home*, 189–209.

6. Eliade discusses the ritualistic return to the womb and its relation to eschatology in *Myth and Reality*, 79–88.

Chapter Six: Toni Morrison, *Sula*

1. Eliade discusses the conception of the end of the world among non-Western cultures and their cyclic notion of time in *Myth and Reality*.

2. Morrison, *Sula*, 4–5. Subsequent references to the novel are noted parenthetically in the text.

3. In his pioneering study of African religion, Mbiti investigates the significance of death among some African people in *African Religions and Philosophy*, 31–34. Among those literary critics who have focused attention on Africanisms in Morrison's *Sula* are Vashti Lewis, "African Tradition in Toni Morrison's *Sula*," 316–24, and Barthold, *Black Time*, 108–12. See also Weems-Hudson and Samuels, *Toni Morrison*, 31–52.

4. Morrison mentions the oneness between Nel and Sula in "Complexity: Toni Morrison's Women," 253.

Chapter Seven: Gloria Naylor, *The Women of Brewster Place*

1. Naylor, *The Women of Brewster Place*, 4–5. Subsequent references to the novel are noted parenthetically in the text.

2. According to Franklin, hostility against white merchants and landlords led to the 1935 Harlem race riot. *From Slavery to Freedom*, 408–9.

3. Naylor develops fully the element of magical realism in her recent novels, *Mama Day* and *Bailey's Cafe*.

4. Christian makes this point in "Trajectories of Self-Definition," 246.

5. Multiple voices representing a global community of women figure prominently in *Bailey's Cafe*. In the novel's culminating scene, the voices of dispossessed women worldwide call and respond across time and space in the ritualization of George's birth.

6. I am indebted to Mattus for insight into the ending of the text and the novel's relationship to Dr. Martin Luther King Jr.'s well-known address. See "Dream, Deferral, and Closure in *The Women of Brewster Place*," 49–63.

BIBLIOGRAPHY

Abrahams, Roger. *Afro-American Folktales: Stories from Black Traditions in the New World.* New York: Panthenon, 1985.

Allen, Shirley, S. "Religious Symbolism and Psychic Reality in Baldwin's *Go Tell it on the Mountain.* In *Critical Essays on James Baldwin,* edited by Fred Standley and Nancy Burt. Boston: G. K. Hall, 1988.

Andrews, Larry R. "Black Sisterhood in Gloria Naylor's Novels." *College Language Association Journal* 33, no. 1 (September 1989): 1–25.

Andrews, William. *The Literary Career of Charles W. Chesnutt.* Baton Rouge: Louisiana State University Press, 1980.

———. *Long Black Song: Essays in Black American Literature and Culture.* Charlottesville: University Press of Virginia, 1972.

Baldwin, James. *The Fire Next Time.* New York: Dial Press, 1963.

———. *Go Tell It on the Mountain.* New York: Dell, 1953.

———. *Notes of a Native Son.* Boston: Beacon Press, 1955.

Barthold, Bonnie. *Black Time: Fiction of Africa, the Caribbean, and the United States.* New Haven: Yale University Press, 1981.

Bell, Bernard W. *The Afro-American Novel and Its Tradition.* Amherst: University of Massachusetts Press, 1987.

Benston, Kimberly W. *Baraka: The Renegade and the Mask.* New Haven: Yale University Press, 1976.

Blassingame, John. *The Slave Community: Plantation Life in the Antebellum South.* New York: Oxford University Press, 1972.

Bone, Robert. *The Negro Novel in America.* New Haven: Yale University Press, 1966.

Brown, Lloyd. "LeRoi Jones [Imamu Amiri Baraka] as Novelist: Theme and Structure in *The System of Dante's Hell.*" *Negro American Literature Forum* 7, no. 4 (Winter 1973): 132–42.

Charles, R. H. *Studies in the Apocalypse.* New York: Scribners, 1913.

Chesnutt, Charles. *The Marrow of Tradition*. Ann Arbor: University of Michigan Press, 1969.

Chesnutt, H. M. *Charles Waddell Chesnutt: Pioneer of the Color Line*. Chapel Hill: University of North Carolina Press, 1952.

Christian, Barbara. "Trajectories of Self-Definition: Placing Contemporary Afro-American Women's Fiction." In *Conjuring: Black Women, Fiction, and Literary Tradition*, edited by Marjorie Pryse and Hortense Spillers. Bloomington: Indiana University Press, 1985.

Cone, James. *Black Theology and Black Power*. New York: Seabury Press, 1969.

————. *The Spirituals and the Blues: An Interpretation*. New York: Seabury Press, 1972.

Dance, Daryl. *Shuckin' and Jivin': Folklore from Contemporary Black Americans*. Bloomington: Indiana University Press, 1978.

Douglass, Frederick. *Narrative of the Life of Frederick Douglass, An American Slave*. Boston: Anti-Slavery Office, 1845.

Du Bois, W. E. B. *The Souls of Black Folk*. New York: New American Library, 1969.

Dundes, Alan, ed. *Mother Wit from the Laughing Barrel: Readings in the Interpretation of Afro-American Folklore*. New York: Garland, 1981.

Eliade, Mircea. *Myth and Reality*. New York: Harper and Row, 1963.

Ellison, Ralph. *Invisible Man*. New York: Random House, 1972.

————. *Shadow and Act*. New York: Random House, 1964.

Fabre, Michel. "Fathers and Sons in James Baldwin's *Go Tell It on the Mountain*." In *James Baldwin, A Collection of Critical Essays*, edited by Keneth Kinnamon. Englewood Cliffs, N.J.: Prentice-Hall, 1974.

Fisher, Myles Mark. *Negro Slave Songs in the United States*. New York: Citadel, 1969.

Franklin, John Hope. *From Slavery to Freedom: A History of Negro Americans*. New York: Knopf, 1974.

Frazier, E. Franklin. *The Negro Church in America*. New York: Schocken, 1963.

Frye, Northrup. *The Anatomy of Criticism*. Princeton: Princeton University Press, 1957.

————. *The Great Code: The Bible and Literature*. New York: Harcourt Brace Jovanovich, 1981.

Gates, Henry Louis. *The Signifying Monkey: A Theory of African-American Literary Criticism*. New York: Oxford University Press, 1988.

Gayle, Addison. *The Black Aesthetic*. Garden City, N.Y.: Doubleday, 1971.

————. *The Way of the New World: The Black Novel in America*. Garden City, N.Y.: Anchor, 1976.

Harris, Trudier. *Black Women in the Fiction of James Baldwin*. Knoxville: University of Tennessee Press, 1985.

————. *Fiction and Folklore: The Novels of Toni Morrison*. Knoxville: University of Tennessee Press, 1991.

Herskovitz, Melville. *The Myth of the Negro Past*. New York: Oxford University Press, 1924.

Horowitz, Floyd. "Ralph Ellison's Modern Version of Brer Bear and Brer Rabbit in *Invisible Man*." *MidContinent Studies Journal* 4, no. 2 (Fall 1963): 21–27.

Howard-Pitney, David. *The Afro-American Jeremiad: Appeals for Justice in America.* Philadelphia: Temple University Press, 1990.

Howe, Irving. "James Baldwin: At Ease in Apocalypse." In *A Collection of Critical Essays,* edited by Keneth Kinnamon. Englewood Cliffs, N.J.: Prentice-Hall, 1974.

Johnson, James Weldon, and J. Rosamond Johnson, eds. *The Books of American Negro Spirituals.* New York: Viking, 1969.

Jones, LeRoi. *Home: Social Essays.* New York: Morrow, 1966.

———. *The System of Dante's Hell.* New York: Grove, 1963.

Joyce, Joyce Ann. *Richard Wright's Art of Tragedy.* Iowa City: University of Iowa Press, 1986.

Kermode, Frank. *The Sense of an Ending.* New York: Oxford University Press, 1967.

Kinnamon, Keneth, ed. *James Baldwin: A Collection of Critical Essays.* Englewood Cliffs, N.J.: Prentice-Hall, 1974.

———. *The Emergence of Richard Wright.* Urbana: University of Illinois Press, 1972.

Leach, Maria, ed. *The Rainbow Book of American Folktales and Legends.* New York: World, 1958.

Lee, Robert A. "Sight and Mask: Ralph Ellison's Invisible Man." *Negro American Literature Forum* 4, no. 1 (March 1970): 22–33.

Lester, Julius. *Black Folktales.* New York: Grove, 1969.

Levine, Lawrence W. *Black Culture and Black Consciousness: Afro-American Folk Thought from Slavery to Freedom.* New York: Oxford University Press, 1977.

Lewis, R. W. B. *Trials of the Word: Essays in American Literature and the Humanistic Tradition.* New Haven: Yale University Press, 1965.

Lewis, Vashti. "African Tradition in Toni Morrison's *Sula.*" In *Wild Women in the Whirlwind: Afro-American Culture and the Contemporary Literary Renaissance,* edited by Joanne Braxton and Andree McLaughlin. New Brunswick, N.J.: Rutgers University Press, 1990.

Littlejohn, David. *Black on White: A Critical Survey of Writing by American Negroes.* New York: Viking, 1969.

Macksey, Richard and Frank E. Moorer, eds. *Richard Wright: A Collection of Critical Essays.* Englewood Cliffs, N.J.: Prentice-Hall, 1984.

Margolies, Edward. *Native Sons: A Critical Study of Twentieth-Century Negro American Authors.* New York: Lippincott, 1968.

Mattus, Jill. "Dream, Deferral, and Closure in *The Women of Brewster Place.*" *Black American Literature Forum* 24, no. 1 (Spring 1990): 49–63.

May, John R. *Toward a New Earth: Apocalypse in the American Novel.* Notre Dame: University of Notre Dame Press, 1972.

Mbiti, John. *African Religions and Philosophy.* Garden City, N.Y.: Doubleday, 1969.

———. *New Testament Eschatology in an African Background.* New York: Oxford University Press, 1971.

Morrison, Toni. *Sula.* New York: Knopf, 1973.

———. "Rootedness: The Ancestor as Foundation." In *Black Women Writers: A Critical Evaluation,* edited by Mari Evans. Garden City, N.Y.: Anchor, 1983.

Moses, Wilson Jeremiah. *Black Messiahs and Uncle Toms: Literary and Social Manipulations of a Religious Myth.* University Park: Pennsylvania University Press, 1982.

Naylor, Gloria. "A Conversation." *Southern Review* 21, no. 3 (July 1985): 567–93.

———. *The Women of Brewster Place.* New York: Penguin, 1982.

O'Neale, Sondra A. "Fathers, Gods, and Religion: Perceptions of Christianity and Ethnic Faith in James Baldwin." In *Critical Essays on James Baldwin*, edited by Fred Standley and Nancy Burt. Boston: G. K. Hall, 1988.

O'Meally, Robert. *The Craft of Ralph Ellison.* Cambridge, Mass.: Harvard University Press, 1980.

Parker, Bettye J. "Complexity: Toni Morrison's Women—An Interview Essay." In *Sturdy Black Bridges: Visions of Black Women in Literature*, edited by Roseann P. Bell, Bettye J. Parker, and Beverly Guy-Sheftall. Garden City, N.Y.: Anchor, 1979.

Raboteau, Albert. *Slave Religion: The Invisible Institution in the Antebellum South.* New York: Oxford University Press, 1980.

Render, Sylvia Lyons. *Charles W. Chesnutt.* Boston: Twayne, 1980.

Roberts, John W. *From Trickster to Badman: The Black Folk Hero in Slavery and Freedom.* Philadelphia: University of Pennsylvania Press, 1989.

Robinson, Douglas. *American Apocalypses: The Image of the End of the World in the American Novel.* Baltimore: Johns Hopkins University Press, 1985.

Russell, D. S. *Apocalyptic: Ancient and Modern.* Philadelphia: Fortress Press, 1978.

Scott, Nathan. "A Search for Beliefs: Richard Wright." *University of Kansas City Review* 23, no. 2 (Fall 1956): 131–38.

Smitherman, Geneva. *Talkin and Testifyin: The Language of Black America.* Detroit: Wayne State University Press, 1977.

Singh, Raman K. "Christian Heroes and Anti-Heroes in Richard Wright's Fiction." *Negro American Literature Forum* 6, no. 4 (Winter 1972): 90–104.

———. "Some Basic Ideas and Ideals in Richard Wright's Fiction," *College Language Association Journal* 13, no. 1 (September 1969): 78–84.

Standley, Fred, and Louis Pratt, eds. *Conversations with James Baldwin.* Jackson: University Press of Mississippi, 1989.

Thomas, H. Nigel. *From Folklore to Fiction: A Study of Folk Heroes and Rituals in the Black American Novel.* New York: Greenwood Press, 1988.

Wade-Gayles, Gloria. *No Crystal Stair: Visions of Race and Sex in Black Women's Fiction.* New York: Pilgrim Press, 1984.

Washington, Booker T. *Up From Slavery.* New York: Dell, 1965.

Willis, Susan. *Specifying: Black Women Writing the American Experience.* Madison: University of Wisconsin Press, 1987.

Wright, Richard. *Black Boy.* New York: Harper and Row, 1993.

———. "Blueprint for Negro Literature." In *Amistad 2: Writings on Black History and Culture*, edited by John A. Williams and Charles F. Harris. New York: Random House, 1971.

———. *Native Son.* New York: Harper and Row, 1940.

INDEX

black arts, LeRoi Jones on, 64, 69

Black Culture and Black Consciousness, 10

Black Power Movement, 97

Black Revolutionary Movement, apocalyptic vision in, 12-13

Black women's movement, emergence of, 97-98; Naylor's use of, in *Women of Brewster Place*, 101-2, 106

Blassingame, John, 8

blindness motif, in Wright's *Native Son*, 29-30

"Block Party, The," 101

"Blueprint for Negro Literature," 3

Blues, Ideology, and Afro-American Literature, 44

Bone, Robert, 56, 61

Bottom communities, motif of, Jones' use of, in *System of Dante's Hell*, 70-73; in Morrison's *Sula*, 74-79

Brearly, H. C., 19-20, 104

Bush, George, 1

Busia, Abena, 100

castration imagery, in *Go Tell It on the Mountain*, 55

chaos imagery, in Ellison's *Invisible Man*, 41, 47-49; in Jones' *System of Dante's Hell*, 67-68; in Morrison's *Sula*, 74-79

Charles, R. H., 6

Chesnutt, Charles, 13-27; apocalyptic vision of, 18-19, 27; badman hero characterization of, 19-20, 104; deconstruction of Washington's utopian vision, 24-27; on purposes of his writing, 26; Washingtonian idealism and, 24-27

Christianity, African-American slave culture and, 7-11; apocalyptic vision in, 6-7; Baldwin's work influenced by, 52-63; images of, in Wright's *Native Son*, 37-38, 104; Jones' distrust of, 67-68

Civil Rights Movement, apocalyptic vision in, 12; origins of, 97

class structure, Ellison's portrayal of, in *Invisible Man*, 43-44, 50-51; Wright's interpretation of, 29-36

color imagery, in *Go Tell It on the Mountain*, 57

Communism, Ellison's work linked with, 46; Wright's exploration of, 31-33, 35-36, 104

community, estrangement from, in Morrison's *Sula*, 80-84; role of, in *Women of Brewster Place*, 96-100

"Complexity: Toni Morrison's Women," 81

Cone, James, 11

Conjure Woman, The, 15-16

Dance, Daryl, 19

Dante, 64, 66

deception, images of, in *Invisible Man*, 40-49

Douglass, Frederick, 2, 9, 49

dream imagery, in *Women of Brewster Place*, 98

drowning imagery, in Morrison's *Sula*, 85

dualism, in African-American fiction, 4, 103

Du Bois, W. E. B., 1, 9, 61

Dunbar, Paul Laurence, 16-17

education in America, Jones' indictment of, 67

"Eighth Ditch, The," 70

Eliade, Mircea, 10, 78, 106

Ellison, Ralph, apocalypse in fiction of, 5, 40-51; folklore used by, 3; political ideologies in work of, 13; on recursive structure of *Invisible Man*, 43-44, 105; on Rinehart's role in *Invisible Man*, 48

Eschatology, African-American interpretations of, 10-12; reversal of, in *Go Tell It on the Mountain*, 600

"Essay on Alice Walker, An," 97

"Ethics of Living Jim Crow, The," 32

"Everyday Use," 93

family relations, Chesnutt's use of in *Marrow of Tradition*, 16

female bonding, in Morrison's *Sula*, 79-84; in *Women of Brewster Place*, 90-96, 100-2

fiction, apocalyptic vision in, 7

Fiction and Folklore, 76
"Fire and Cloud," 32
fire imagery, in Go Tell It on the Mountain,
    60-61; in Wright's Native Son, 33-36
Fire Next Time, The, 53, 63
flight metaphor, in Jones' System of Dante's
    Hell, 69-70; in Wright's Native Son, 30-
    31
folklore. See also spirituals; African-
    American novelists' use of, 3-5;
    Chesnutt's use of, 15-17, 20-21;
    Ellison's use of, in Invisible Man, 42,
    46; image of, in Wright's Native Son,
    30-31; in Morrison's Sula, 75-77, 81-
    82, 85-87; in Women of Brewster Place,
    88-96
Frazier, E. Franklin, 8-9
"Freedom and Apocalypse: A Thematic
    Approach to Black Expression," 2
Frye, Northrup, 7, 99

Garvey, Marcus, 12, 47, 79
Gates, Henry Louis, 4, 105
Gayle, Addison Jr., 17-18, 41, 64
"God Manifest," Jewish apocalyptic
    vision and, 6
Go Tell It on the Mountain, apocalyptic vision
    in, 52-63; conversion experience in,
    53-58; father-son relationship in, 56-
    57; Pentecostal Church as voice in,
    58-60; ritual cleansing and purifica-
    tion in, 60-63
Griggs, Sutton, 27

"Harlem," 97
Harris, Trudier, 62, 76
Hasidim, apocalyptic vision of, 6
heaven, slaves' conception of, 10, 103
Herskovitz, Melville J., 8
Holloway, Karla, 101
Home, 67, 69
homosexuality in, in Jones' System of
    Dante's Hell, 70
Howard-Pitney, David, 11
"How Bigger Was Born," 34
Hughes, Langston, 97

Imperium in Imperio, 27
Inferno, 64, 66, 68
Invisible Man, apocalyptic vision in, 49-
    51; Brer Rabbit imagery in, 46-47;
    Brotherhood motif in, 46-47; Golden
    Day incident in, 44-45; oral tradition
    in, 49-51; recursive structure of, 43-
    44, 105; Rinehart's role in, 48-49;
    tricksters, confidence men and
    antichrists in, 40-49

JanMohammed, Abdul R., 4, 65
John of Patmos, 6
Johnson, James Weldon, 9
Jones, LeRoi, apocalyptic vision in work
    of, 12, 64-73; on black arts, 64, 69
Joyce, Joyce Ann, 32
Judaism, apocalyptic vision in, 5-6,
    103; motifs of, in Women of Brewster
    Place, 91-92

Kermode, Frank, 7, 73
King, Martin Luther Jr., 12

language, usage patterns of African-
    Americans, 9-10
"Last Days of the American Empire,
    The," 12
Lee, A. Robert, 43
lesbianism, in Women of Brewster Place,
    100-2
Levine, Lawrence, 8, 10
Lewis, R. W. B., 40, 48
Linden Hills, 101
Long Black Song, 2, 32
lynching, as motif in Chesnutt's fiction,
    17

manhood, economic empowerment
    linked to, in Wright's Native Son, 31; as
    motif in Chesnutt's Marrow of Tradition,
    18-20; as motif in Morrison's Sula,
    78-79
"Man Who Lived Underground, The,"
    38
Marrow of Tradition, The, 13-27

matriarchal images, in Morrison's *Sula*,
78-79; in *Women of Brewster Place*, 98-
100
Mbiti, John, 10, 106
Midsummer Night's Dream, A, 98-99
Moorings and Metaphors, 101
Morrison, Toni, 14; apocalyptic imagery
in *Sula*, 74-87; female bonding and
quest for wholeness in work of, 79-
84
Moses, Wilson Jeremiah, 11
mother-daughter relationships, in *Women
of Brewster Place*, 90-96
music. *See also* spirituals

Native Son, apocalyptic vision in, 36-39;
color symbolism in, 34; fire imagery
in, 33-34; religious discourse in, 33-
34; vision of racial armageddon in,
28-36
Naylor, Gloria, 14; apocalyptic vision of,
88-102; Hughes' poetry used by, 97;
treatment of lesbianism by, 100-2
Negro Church in America, The, 8
"Neutrals: the Vestibule," 66
news media, race antagonism perpetuated by, 18
*New Testament Eschatology in an African
Background*, 10
"new world order," conflicting visions
of, 1
"Ninth Ditch: the Makers of Discord,
The," 67-68
Notes of a Native Son, 57
novels by African-Americans, apocalypse
in, 2-3, 103

oral tradition, apocalypse in African
American traditions, 2-3, 8;
Baldwin's use of, in *Go Tell It on the
Mountain*, 58-63; Ellison's use of, in
Invisible Man, 42, 44, 49-51; in Jones'
System of Dante's Hell, 64; spirituals as
part of, 9-10; in *Women of Brewster Place*,
101-2
origins, pilgrimage to, in Morrison's
Sula, 84-87

Outsider, The, 38

patriarchy, in *Go Tell It on the Mountain*, 62-
63; in *Women of Brewster Place*, 94-96
Pentecostal Church, as motif in
Baldwin's *Go Tell It on the Mountain*, 52-
63
Pryse, Marjorie, 89
purification rites, Baldwin's use of, in *Go
Tell It on the Mountain*, 60-63

Raboteau, Albert, 8-9
rebirth imagery, in Morrison's *Sula*, 81;
in *Women of Brewster Place*, 91-92
Revelation, Book of, apocalyptic vision
in, 6-7
ritual cleansings, Baldwin's use of, in *Go
Tell It on the Mountain*, 60-63; in *Women of
Brewster Place*, 99-100
"Rootedness: The Ancestor as Foundation," 79
Russell, D. S., 5-6, 13

Satanic imagery, in *Invisible Man*, 48; in
Morrison's *Sula*, 84; in Wright's *Native
Son*, 38-39
selfhood, Jones on development of, 70-
72; quest for wholeness in
Morrison's *Sula* and, 79-84; violence
as vehicle for, in Wright's *Native Son*,
37-39
sermonic discourse, Baldwin's use of, in
Go Tell It on the Mountain, 59-60; role of,
in African-American culture, 11-12;
in *Women of Brewster Place*, 94-96
seven, images of, in Jones' *System of
Dante's Hell*, 73
sexism, in *Go Tell It on the Mountain*, 62-63
sexuality, in Morrison's *Sula*, 80-85; as
motif in Chesnutt's *Marrow of Tradition*,
18-20; in *Women of Brewster Place*, 93-94
Shadow and Act, 42-43, 47-48, 76
Siegel, Paul, 35
Slater, Morris (Railroad Bill) (folk
hero), 22-23
slave culture of African-Americans,
apocalyptic visions in, 7-12; in
Morrison's *Sula*, 75-76

Smitherman, 103

snow imagery, in Wright's *Native Son*, 34-35

"Sound and Image," 65

spirituals, role of, in African-American culture, 9-10; in Wright's *Native Son*, 38

Stagolee (folk hero), 21-22

Sula, apocalyptic imagery in, 74-87; Bottom community motif in, 74-79; chaos imagery in, 74-79; female bonding and quest for wholeness in, 79-84

System of Dante's Hell, The, 64-73

Thomas, H. Nigel, 16, 46

"Treachery to Kindred," 68

tricksters and confidence men, Ellison's use of, in *Invisible Man*, 40-49, 105

"two-ness" of black experience, 4, 61

Uncle Tom's Children, 31-33

urban migration, apocalyptic vision in, 12; failure of, in Wright's *Native Son*, 38

utopianism, Chesnutt-Washington controversy over, 24-27; in Wright's *Native Son*, 35

violence, Chesnutt's rejection of, 23-24; as vehicle for selfhood, in Wright's *Native Son*, 37-39

Wade-Gayles, Gloria, 94, 97

Walker, Alice, 93, 97

Walker, David, 11-12

Washington, Booker T., 24-27, 45, 49-50

Washington, Mary Helen, 97

Way of the New World, The, 17-18

Willis, Susan, 3

Wilmington race riot of 1898, fictionalization of, in Chesnutt's *Marrow of Tradition*, 15

Women of Brewster Place, The, apocalyptic vision of, 88-102; urban folk community in, 88-96; wall imagery in, 96-100

Women's Liberation Movement, 97

women's roles, in Morrison's *Sula*, 80-83

World War II, evolution of civil rights and, 97

Wright, Richard, 3; apocalypse in fiction of, 4, 13-14, 28-39; Baldwin's views on, 56; vision of racial armageddon, 28-36